64 Surefire Strategies for Being Understood When Communicating with Co-Workers

64 Surefire Strategies for Being Understood When Communicating with Co-Workers

Walter St. John

BEP BUSINESS EXPERT PRESS

64 Surefire Strategies for Being Understood When Communicating with Co-Workers

First published in 2018 by
Business Expert Press, LLC
222 East 46th Street, New York, NY 10017
www.businessexpertpress.com

ISBN-13: 978-1-94744-157-6 (paperback)
ISBN-13: 978-1-94744-158-3 (e-book)

Business Expert Press Corporate Communication Collection

Collection ISSN: 2156-8162 (print)
Collection ISSN: 2156-8170 (electronic)

Cover and interior design by Exeter Premedia Services Private Ltd., Chennai, India

First edition: 2018

10 9 8 7 6 5 4 3 2 1

Printed in the United States of America.

Abstract

One of the most difficult challenges encountered daily by managers throughout their careers is getting what they say understood by their coworkers.

The purpose of this book is to provide practicing and aspiring managers, as well as students of management, with a practical and comprehensive reference for being understood when communicating with their coworkers and those they manage.

64 Surefire Strategies for Being Understood when Communicating with Co-Workers is organized into seven chapters:

1. Personality Traits
2. Organization of the Message
3. Content of the Message
4. Context of the Message
5. Word and Language Use
6. Clarifying the Message
7. Speaking Voice and Style

In addition, the book offers a self-assessment of communicating skills related to getting what you say understood. This assessment provides valuable insights into your communicating strengths and weaknesses.

The book identifies the main factors that influence a speaker's and writer's ability to get understood and explains how you can use each of these factors to better connect with your listeners and readers.

Here are several key points about the organization and content of this book:

1. Each factor is defined in the first paragraph for each topic
2. An explanation is then offered for the way each factor is used to promote understanding
3. The information is practical rather than theoretical
4. The writing style is informal instead of scholarly
5. The information is specific and presented in a simple, direct, and no-nonsense manner

6. All topics are presented in a concise manner using bullets to list and identify the various ideas offered
7. The information applies to communicating with both individuals and groups
8. Each topic can be read quickly and is designed to save the reader time

It needs to be emphasized that all managers have the ability to improve how they communicate with their coworkers. The information contained in this book will help managers say the right thing, in the right way, and at the right time when interacting with their coworkers.

Keywords

communicating strategies, comprehension, connecting, managerial communications, meaning, talking with coworkers, understanding, feedback

Contents

Introduction ix

Chapter 1   Personality Traits 1

Chapter 2   Organization of the Message 27

Chapter 3   Content of the Message 33

Chapter 4   Context of a Message 45

Chapter 5   Word and Language Use 55

Chapter 6   Clarifying the Message 75

Chapter 7   Speaking Voice and Style 97

Appendix A: Self-Assessment of Skills Related to Getting What You Say Understood 115

Appendix B: Self-Assessment of Skills Related to Understanding What Is Said to You 119

About the Author 123

Index 125

Introduction

We have all felt the happiness and satisfaction from getting understood by another person. Conversely, we have felt the frustration and sense of futility when that fails to happen.

Tragically, one of the most difficult challenges we encounter throughout our lives is getting what we say understood. Family members, friends, and business associates all struggle to get what they are saying understood.

Many obstacles exist that interfere with the achievement of mutual understanding. These barriers include differences in age, gender, race, ethnicity, religion, nationality, culture, occupations, educational levels, beliefs, perceptions, attitudes, and intelligence.

Regrettably, despite its importance, the ability to gain understanding between people too often remains only a distant hope rather than a reality.

The purpose of this book is to give you practical and specific ways to connect with coworkers. The ideas presented should help you to say the right things, in the right way at the right time.

The book identifies the major factors that influence a speaker's ability to get understood and explains how he/she can use each of these factors to connect with their listeners.

The suggestions offered are intended to apply whether you are speaking to an individual or group.

The constant and pervasive goal of all communication is to gain mutual understanding. You will enhance your communication if you keep in mind that every message that you send has three components that need to be used effectively: (1) the content, (2) your voice tone, and (3) your body language. All three of these elements need to be complementary and consistent with each other if your message is to be interpreted accurately. It is vital that you, as the person speaking, accept the primary responsibility for getting understood. Here are several points about the organization of this book:

- The content includes 64 separate and distinct factors that influence understanding between the person speaking and person listening. Several of these factors are related and may appear to overlap one another, but they actually contain differences worth noting.

- Each factor is defined in the first paragraph. Next, an explanation is offered for how such factor should be used to promote understanding.
- The information is practical rather than theoretical and is presented with an informal rather than scholarly style.
- Each topic is offered in a concise manner to save you time.

All topics can be read in short time spurts rather than requiring extended reading time.

You definitely have the ability to improve the way you communicate with people.

You can connect with people!

We wish you success in your efforts to connect with people in a mutually rewarding manner.

CHAPTER 1

Personality Traits

Have an Appealing Personality

Don't give yourself airs! Do you think I can listen all day to such stuff?
Be off, or I'll kick you downstairs.

—Humpty Dumpty (from Alice in Wonderland)

A person's personality is his or her total behavior and emotional characteristics. All these characteristics combined distinguish an individual and group from other individuals and groups.

You are Your Message! Your personality is your most important means of communicating with people as it can make them receptive to or reject what you say to them. Therefore, you need to be careful that your personality enhances rather than detracts from your message. It is important to realize that sometimes there is so much of the person in his or her message that their personality interferes with their message. When this happens, your listeners are distracted and concentrate on the speaker instead of what he or she is saying. As the saying goes, "How can I hear what you are saying when there is so much of you saying it?"

It can't be emphasized too much that what matters most to your listeners is who you are. They are influenced only second most by how you are saying what you are saying and third most by the content (what) of your message. Yes, it is your speaking style (the how) that is most important to most of your listeners than the substance (the what) of your presentation.

You reveal your personality to people in four ways: (1) your appearance, (2) your choice of words, (3) your voice tone, and (4) your body language. Each of these factors is dealt with as separate topics through the book.

The following is a list of desirable personality characteristics for speakers to display when speaking to individuals or groups:

- Friendly, warm, and approachable
- Sincere, honest, and trustworthy
- Genuine, real, and authentic
- Open-minded, adaptable, and flexible
- Positive attitude balanced with a realistic outlook on things
- Integrity along with high ethical standards
- Enthusiasm for both the topic and the listeners
- Confident, assured, and poised
- Modest, unassuming, and down-to-earth
- Candid, straightforward, and plain-spoken
- Sensitive and aware of other people's needs and desires
- "You" (other person) centered rather than "I" and "me" centered

Create a Feeling of Commonality

. . . but common interests will always prevail.

—unknown

Commonality refers to relating something familiar or that is known to people generally. It is having something a speaker has in common or shares with his or her listeners.

Your listeners will be more comfortable with you and open to our ideas when your ideas are compatible with their own. People will understand you more when the information you are sharing is consistent with their own beliefs, attitudes, and experiences. Therefore, it is imperative that you share the things you have in common with them (and the sooner you do this in your talk the better).

Your goal is to create a sense of unity and togetherness with your listeners. There are an almost endless number of ways that you can do this. These include:

cultural background	ethnic origin	occupations
educational background	nationality	age
lifestyle	leisure-time pursuits	interests
language spoken	gender	likes and dislikes

beliefs and attitudes	family	health issues
experiences	regions lived in	problems faced
travel	affiliations	religion

Here are several proven ways that will help you to develop a feeling of commonality with the people you are conversing with:

- Stress as many similarities as possible between you and your listeners.
- Emphasize areas of agreement and downplay areas of disagreement.
- Strive to agree in principle even if your opinions on the details differ.
- Use we lots and I and me little.
- Preface your statements as follows whenever you can:
  1. As we both know …
  2. As we can both agree …
  3. We share the same beliefs that …
- Refer to well-known people that are liked and respected by your listeners.
- Quote people your listeners know and admire.
- Cite local events, situations, and examples.
- Tell stories of mutual interest.
- Use examples closely related to the lives of your listeners.
- Demonstrate that you know important things about your listeners.
- Smile often and show your listeners you like them and appreciate the opportunity to be with them.
- Use words that have a positive impact on people.
- Tell something personal about yourself, including some mistakes you have made (show that you are human).
- Talk your listeners' lingo if it is natural for you to do so (don't talk like you are from Boston when you are talking with people from Atlanta or like a professor when talking with people from humble backgrounds).

Demonstrate the Right Attitude

A merry heart doeth good like medicine.

—Proverbs 17:22

Your attitude is your predisposition to feel favorably or unfavorably toward a person, object, or event.

An attitude can't be observed directly; instead, it is something that must be inferred from a person's behavior. People convey their attitudes through their appearance, verbal comments, voice tone, and body language.

Your attitude is tremendously important because it influences your relations and communication with people. Your attitude can help or hinder your ability to get understood. You need to have the right attitude to communicate anything effectively. You are in charge of your own attitude and have the option to display either a positive or a negative attitude toward yourself and your listeners as well as the subject you are talking about.

Try to be optimistic about your ability to connect with people. By being optimistic and positive you will help people to feel at ease with you and consequently more receptive to your message.

Mahatma Gandhi made these powerful points about positive thinking:

Keep your thoughts positive because your thoughts become your words. Keep your words positive because your words become your behaviors. Keep your behaviors positive because your behaviors become your habits. Keep your habits positive because your habits become your values. Keep your values positive because your values become your destiny.

The following attitudes will assist you to get your message understood by people:

- Be friendly and show you like and respect your listeners.
- Stress "you" and "we" when talking with people and downplay the use of "I" and "me."
- Learn something important about your listeners to avoid labeling or stereotyping them.

- Be sure to treat your listeners as equals.
- Demonstrate confidence balanced with modesty while talking. Sound as though you know what you are talking about without being condescending. Above all, avoid coming across as a know-it-all. Express yourself simply and use words that are easy to understand.
- Be realistic about your listeners' knowledge and interest in the subject (neither over- nor underestimate these.)
- Be patient with and considerate of your listeners. If they don't understand you right away, it is best to refrain from showing any irritation and saying anything critical. Instead, simply state what you want to say in another way.
- Expect the best from your listeners and show that you enjoy being with them.
- Convey an attitude that you are merely sharing information with your listeners rather than lecturing them.
- Show that the important thing is not you but what you are saying. You want to avoid having your listeners ask themselves, "How can I hear what you are saying when there is so much of you saying it?"

Desire to Get Understood

Man's painful desire to communicate without coalescing.
—Clifton Fadiman

A person's desire is his or her wish or want for something. It also means a longing or craving for something.

No one can communicate effectively without the desire to do so. The first step toward getting understood is the desire to be understood.

The desire to be understood requires that you be willing to reveal your true thoughts and feelings about things. Desire also demands that you accept the responsibility for and consequences for anything you disclose. A true desire to get understood also means that you are committed to giving what you say the necessary time and effort to make it comprehensible to people.

The strength of your desire to attain understanding is based on the following factors:

1. Your views toward the subject—it must be genuinely important to you
2. You consider the occasion itself so important that you feel it is imperative to get your ideas across accurately
3. Your attitude toward yourself—you need to believe that getting understood is important to your image and reputation
4. Your attitude toward your listeners—you must consider them to be valuable, worthwhile, and important people

Make a Genuine Effort to Get Understood

Keep the faculty of effort alive in you by a little gratuitous exercise every day.

——William James

When you make an effort to get what you say understood, you consciously exert energy to do so. Effort involves making a serious and deliberate attempt to get understood. Getting yourself understood doesn't just happen; it requires desire, strong effort, and hard work.

The person speaking is expected to make a concerted effort to get understood. This is his or her responsibility. It is presumptuous to expect your listeners to make a strong effort to understand what you are saying.

You make an effort to get understood by:

- Thinking carefully about what you need to say in advance
- Learning important things about your listeners ahead of time
- Concentrating 100 percent on what you are saying and blocking out any distractions
- Having your body language support everything you are saying
- Taking the time to adapt your content, wording, and speaking style to the people listening to you
- Securing feedback from your listeners' facial expressions, posture, body movement, and questions

Be Aware of Other People

An unexamined life is not worth living.

—Socrates

Awareness exists when a person perceives and has knowledge of something.

Your message will be better understood if you can achieve congruence between how you view things and how your listeners view them. Unless you and your listeners have the same frame of reference, misunderstandings are likely to occur. Do your best to imagine how life looks to your listeners so that you can adapt what you say and how you say it based on this awareness.

When your awareness is accurate and based on reality, you will connect with people better because you can deal with them as they actually are rather than what you mistakenly thought they were.

It is also important to become aware of how you and your subject are perceived by the people listening to you.

Here are several vital things to know regarding awareness that will assist you to get understood:

- Your perception of things is based on your culture, past experiences, self-concept, beliefs, interests, prejudices, and mood at a certain time.
- Every human being has a unique and different awareness of life, people, objects, and events. No two people see things exactly the same way. As Dr. Konrad Adenauer stated so insightfully: We all live under the same sky, but we don't all have the same horizon.
- We are limited in our ability to perceive things. It is simply impossible to be aware of everything. We are able to be aware of only a small part of what exists and is going on and around us.
- Our perceptions are selective. We pay attention to certain events, people, and information and ignore others. In addition, we tend to see and hear what we expect and want to see and hear (e.g., when listening to presidential debates).

- We tend to tune out information that conflicts with our beliefs and expectations. As Ralph Waldo Emerson so aptly put it: "Some things have to be believed to be seen."
- One person's reality is pure fantasy to someone else.
- Since differences in perception are inevitable and so widespread, it is important that you avoid making the mistake of assuming that the way you perceive things is accurate and the same as others view them—it simply ain't so. For example, three people viewing the Grand Canyon might comment thusly:
  1. A clergyman: "One of the wonders of God."
  2. An archaeologist: "What a wonder of science!"
  3. A cowboy: "What a heck of a place to lose a cow!"

You will understand other people better if you become aware of their ages, gender, educational level, cultural background, personalities, occupations, group affiliations, and geographical areas living and lived in, as well as their knowledge, attitudes, and interest in the subject being discussed.

You can become aware of important things about people by:

- Learning about the topics they talk about
- Finding out how they spend their time
- Asking them questions about themselves
- Asking their friends and associates about them
- Discovering their interests
- Noting the things they have strong feelings about
- Observing the kinds of words they use
- Identifying the groups they are affiliated with
- Watching their facial expressions and body language while you are talking with them

Feel and Show Empathy

We have not really budged a step until we take up residence in someone else's point of view.

—John Erskine

Empathetic speakers are aware of and sensitive to the views, thoughts, feelings, and experiences of their listeners. A person is empathetic when he or she is free of making judgments about other people and accepts them for what they are. The word compassion is often used interchangeably with empathy.

Understanding is increased when the person speaking and the person listening have empathy for each other. Mutual understanding is aided by mutual empathy.

By showing empathy for your listeners you help develop rapport, which further promotes their willingness to try to understand what you are saying. A speaker who is liked creates greater receptivity to his or her message and thus the listeners try harder to understand what is being said.

You can show empathy for the thoughts and feelings of your listeners by:

- Finding out what is important to them
- Demonstrating you value them as people and consider them to be important to you
- Acting friendly and showing that you like them
- Using appropriate and respectful words
- Talking about things interesting and important to them
- Encouraging them to state their ideas and reactions to your comments freely

Be Candid

Truth is never pure and rarely simple.

—Oscar Wilde

Being candid means being sincere and straightforward when you talk with people. It is being free of bias and deception. Synonyms for candid are honesty and frankness. It is important to realize that the basis for any good relationship is honesty and candid communication.

When being candid, you have the choice of being frank and saying something as it exactly is or toning it down a little to help your listeners feel more comfortable with what you are saying. It is best to be candid without being brutally frank. It is often quite a challenge to be both frank and tactful at the same time and still get understood; however, it is possible.

Let people know exactly what is on your mind in terms they can comprehend. Obviously, people can't guess what is on your mind and what you are really trying to say to them.

Let's be realistic—there is risk in saying precisely what you want to say. Frankness can cause the people listening to you to become upset, defensive, and even antagonistic toward you.

It is sometimes contrary to your best interests to be completely frank with people because many people become uncomfortable when exposed to the truth or when you call a spade a spade. Therefore, it is foolish to say everything you really want to say and just let the chips fall where they may.

Consider the consequences before simply blurting out completely what is on your mind. It is wise to always use discretion and consider people's feelings when being frank with them. You gain little and can lose a lot from overkill and dumping a full load on people.

On the other hand, you can cause misunderstandings when you are not completely frank with people and sugar-coat the truth on important matters. Being politically correct can also cause misunderstanding because it says it as it isn't.

Ask yourself these four questions before being candid with anyone:

1. Why do I need to say what I intend on saying?
2. Do I really need to say it?
3. Will saying it make matters better or worse?
4. How can I say it so clearly that my point gets across and yet tactfully enough to minimize offending the other person?

Here are several tips you can benefit from when speaking candidly with people:

- Be aware of people's need to protect themselves psychologically by using various defense mechanisms such as distorting what you are saying or tuning you out totally.

- Have the courage to reveal important things about yourself to build trust.
- Desire to be open and truthful with people.
- Be willing to accept the consequences of being candid.
- Trust your listeners to be open to hearing what you have to say.
- Present the essential facts fairly and objectively.
- Tell people what you want to talk about and explain why it is necessary.
- Balance frankness with tact.

There are certain words and phrases that you should avoid using because they are enemies of candor. These include:

- Wishy-washy words or phrases such as maybe, appears, perhaps, generally, possibly, they say
- Self-protective disclaimers such as "Just off the top of my head I think …" or "I don't know if this will work" when you are confident it will or "Now this is only a guess but …"
- Qualifying phrases such as "It is my understanding . . . ," "It might possibly work," or "Don't quote me on this but …"

Remember, your goal should be to say things as they really are and not as they are not.

Demonstrate Courage

Courage is a virtue only in proportion as it is directed by prudence.
—François de la Monta Fenclon

Courage is defined as the moral strength to persevere and withstand danger or fear. A courageous speaker says what needs to be said, says it candidly and directly, and then accepts the responsibility for what was said.

Some situations require courage for you to say what needs to be said. Understandably, most people are reluctant at times to say what should be said because they don't want to hurt people's feelings or risk being disliked, yet in some situations you have no choice but to bite the bullet and say what needs to be said.

If you don't say what needs to be said candidly and in a straightforward manner, people can't possibly know what you really mean and thus they will fail to understand what you are saying.

When the situation demands that you level with people and state exactly what needs to be said about something, it is wise to first ask yourself these pertinent questions:

- Do I really need to say it?
- How can I best say it?
- When is the best time to say it?
- Am I the best person to say it?
- What will be the consequences if I say it or don't say it?

Unfortunately, employers, parents, spouses, friends, doctors, clerics, police, counselors, and teachers must at times deliver bad news or make critical comments to and about people.

Sometimes they have no other options. The following are several examples that require courage to speak frankly with the people involved. (Ask yourself what would be the result of remaining silent, sugar-coating your comments, or speaking frankly in each instance):

- A doctor having to tell several parents of young children that the child has an incurable disease and death is imminent
- An employer informing a worker that he or she is being laid off when the employer knows the family is living paycheck to paycheck
- Parents telling their young children that they are going to be divorced and the family is going to be split up
- A friend telling a close, lifelong friend that he or she has bad breath and a repugnant body odor
- A police officer needing to inform a wife that her husband has just been killed in a car wreck

Delaying or failing to say what needs to be said in these situations solves nothing and often makes matters worse. These situations demand that you face the situation courageously and say what needs to be said in a straightforward, compassionate manner.

Show Sincerity

No language but the language of the heart.

—Alexander Pope

To be sincere is to be honest, genuine, and heartfelt. There is an absence of hypocrisy, deceit, and subterfuge. A sincere speaker says what he or she honestly thinks, believes, and feels about something. Such individuals share their thoughts fully and candidly without holding anything back when speaking to people.

As a speaker your sincerity is important as it is directly related to your success when speaking. Sincerity lies at the heart of all communication. To appear sincere you must actually be sincere. It is unwise to fake sincerity because most listeners can quickly detect whether or not you are a person with integrity who is speaking with conviction (talking from your heart and not merely with your lips).

Whenever you are insincere, you are sabotaging your speaking efforts because insincere communication is ineffective—it creates resistance to what you are saying. Your goal as a sincere speaker is to reveal and not conceal. It is to share your thoughts and feelings honestly about a subject rather than to hide or disguise them.

By doing the following you will help project your sincerity to people listening to you.

- Speak with conviction—say what you mean, mean what you say, and show that you mean it.
- Be sure your past statements and actions are consistent with what you are currently saying and doing.
- Know what you are talking about—don't bluff or guess when answering questions. If you don't know the answer

to a question, simply say "I don't know." Better yet, say "I don't know but I will find out for you and get back to you by next week."

- Act natural and genuine—avoid putting on airs or displaying any affectation.
- Smile with a full and lingering smile rather than with a half or fleeting smile.
- Say the same thing with your words, facial expressions, body movement, and voice tone (you need to send a consistent message).
- Speak without undue hesitation and without saying anything contradictory.
- Maintain steady eye contact with your listeners.
- Avoid having a hidden agenda behind your actual comments.

Create Rapport

Treat others as they want to be treated, not as you want to be treated.
—Anonymous

Rapport exists when harmony is present between people and when they get along well together. It exists when people like and have an affinity for each other.

Rapport is the foundation for all successful relationships and communication. Rapport is to communication what gasoline is to a car. The feelings of your listeners toward you are important in determining their willingness to listen and to understand your message. People won't try to understand what you are saying unless they like and respect you. If your listeners dislike you, neither your eloquence or style nor your fluency with words will overcome their resistance to your message.

Relational messages exist as well as content messages every time you say something to someone. They demonstrate how the speaker and his or her listeners feel about each other. The closeness of a relationship has a significant impact on how any message is received. Your relationships will be enhanced if you share your feelings as well as your thoughts with the people you are talking with. Your listeners want to know you as a person in order for them to understand you better.

Your goal when speaking to a single individual or a group of people is to develop as much rapport as you can as quickly as possible. Strive to make your listeners immediately receptive to what you have to say.

The following ideas will help you to develop rapport with your listeners:

- Find out what your listeners expect from you and tailor your message to meet these expectations.
- Learn how much your listeners know about the subject.
- Try to see things from your listeners' point of view (let them know you understand their world).
- Use personal touch. Use a lot of personal pronouns (I, we, and you). Stress you and we while downplaying I and me when talking with people.
- Establish common ground. Emphasize your similarities and minimize your differences. Create a feeling of camaraderie and togetherness.
- Make your listeners feel important (we all want to feel important and to be treated like we are somebody).
- Show you appreciate your listeners' abilities and accomplishments.
- Involve your listeners—give them a chance to make comments and ask questions. Also ask semirhetorical questions to give people an opportunity to respond to what you've said (for example, a show of hands).
- Cite examples that relate to your listeners' daily lives.
- Build on your listeners' preexisting beliefs and interests.
- Act enthusiastic and show that you are enjoying yourself. Smile often and big. A smile says I like you and I'm happy to be with you. By smiling you also help your listeners to feel relaxed and comfortable around you.
- Act modest and down-to-earth like a regular person.
- Speak as an equal and play down any differences in status.
- Act natural and show that you are human.
- Don't act like a know-it-all. Be willing to frankly admit mistakes you've made and state "I don't know" to questions rather than bluffing or guessing your answers.

- Speak in a pleasant, conversational tone of voice (be sure not to sound preachy or holier-than-thou).
- Show a sense of humor—have fun and laugh with your listeners.
- Use appealing language. Get on the same wavelength by using familiar words and plain language.
- Use gender-fair and gender-neutral words.

Establish Credibility

I hold that the characteristic of the present age is craving credibility.
—Benjamin Disraeli

Credibility is having the power to gain people's trust and belief in what you are saying. To be viewed as credible you need to be seen as trustworthy, competent, sincere, and well intentioned.

You must have credibility to be believed. People will pay closer attention to what you are saying when they think that you know what you are talking about. Conversely, without credibility your message will be suspect and may even be discounted. Therefore, it is imperative that you give top priority to establishing your credibility.

Your reputation precedes the time when you actually begin speaking to people. Your reputation can be an asset or a liability. Ideally, your reputation will, by itself, show why are you qualified to speak on the topic. In any event, be sure to tell your listeners about your training and experiences regarding your subject at the start of your talk.

If you are speaking to a large group of people, be certain to provide the person assigned to introduce you a succinct list of your most important qualifications for speaking on the topic. In addition, modestly mention additional training and experiences connected to the subject periodically during your presentation.

Your credibility and overall reputation are enhanced when you are sincere and truthful in all that you say. While speaking you want to show a strong sense of ethics and integrity. You further aid your credibility and image when you show that you have made a genuine effort to learn important things about your listeners. You will elicit a positive reception from people when you demonstrate that you not only understand their needs and problems but that you share some of them.

Your appearance and mannerisms are important. People will quickly size you up and form an opinion about you before you utter a word. Be sure to wear clothing appropriate for the occasion and nature of the topic. It is usually best to dress conservatively. Also, look well groomed and refrain from wearing any distracting jewelry. By looking and acting confident you bolster your credibility. It is essential that you act poised and relaxed in order to appear confident.

You express confidence by dressing appropriately, having an erect posture, maintaining steady eye contact, speaking fluently with an assured manner, gesturing frequently and freely, and by inviting questions. You further exhibit confidence by readily stating you don't know something rather than bluffing and by admitting your past mistakes.

On the other hand, you diminish your projection of confidence when you do the following:

- Appear nervous, hesitant, and insincere
- Act tentative, indecisive, and unsure
- Make hedging and qualifying statements or habitually use weasel words such as somewhat, kind of, usually, generally, and possibly
- State frequent disclaimers such as "I'm not really sure," "I'm only guessing but …," and "I could be wrong but …"

Take prolonged pauses or repeatedly make sounds such as ah, em, um, and so forth.

Strive to Be Tactful

Diplomacy is to do and say the nastiest things in the nicest way.
—Isaac Goldberg

Tact is being sensitive to what we say and do in order to maintain good relationships and avoid giving offense to someone. It is saying and doing what is considerate and diplomatic.

Being tactful involves saying and doing the right thing in the right way at the right time. In order to be tactful you need to consider the feelings and viewpoints of other people. In addition, you need to consider the impact and consequences of what you say and do.

One of the realities of life is that the truth hurts sometimes; there is no denying this fact. There are times when you must be candid and say what needs to be said even if it hurts and is distasteful. However, while leveling with someone you need to avoid leveling the person in the process.

The constant challenge is to be tactful even when you have to be "brutally frank." You don't have to be rude to be candid nor lie to be tactful. There is a middle ground. Realize that if you are too tactful or subtle, you may fail to convey what you are actually thinking and feeling and thus your listeners will fail to understand what you are really trying to say.

In order to be tactful, people sometimes use euphemisms (saying gentle and soft words to express stronger and harsher feelings). You need to be careful when using euphemisms because they water down or disguise your true feelings on the matter (the result is that what needs to be said does not get said).

Remember your goal when communicating is to speak plainly and candidly without being abrasive, offending people, and creating resentment.

You can attain your objective of being tactful by:

- Thinking before speaking
- Predicting people's reactions to what you plan to say and modifying what you are going to say accordingly
- Being polite and respectful in all you say and do
- Treating others as important people and as equals
- Speaking honestly and candidly without being unpleasant and insulting
- Saying negative things in a more gentle and considerate way (euphemistically) yet making sure that your listeners get the point (for example, saying that a person made a mistake rather than stating he or she was wrong to do something)
- Using socially acceptable words and avoiding strong and offensive language that unduly antagonizes people (for example, refraining from using profanity or vulgar expressions)

- Describing the problem caused by the person rather than blaming or finding fault with the person himself/herself
- Doing your best to see things from the other person's viewpoint to gain perspective on the situation

Build Trust

Trust, like the soul, never returns once it is gone.

—Publilius Syrus

We trust people who talk to us when we have confidence in them and consider them reliable. We have faith that they are telling us the truth.

Effective communication is based on mutual trust. Trust is essential for harmonious relations. Rapport between the speaker and the listener contributes greatly to gaining mutual understanding. Without basic trust in the speaker, listeners will be reluctant to believe what is being said. When trust exists, suspicions about a speaker are minimized as is the need for the people listening to act defensive and self-protective.

Any speaker who offends, threatens, or diminishes his or her listeners is unlikely to be trusted and thus jeopardizes his or her chances of being understood. Fortunately, there are many ways you can gain the trust of your listeners. These include:

- Having a reputation of being fair, balanced, and objective when presenting information to people
- Building a reputation of being a principled person with integrity
- Having common goals and interests
- Acting open-minded and receptive to new ideas and divergent opinions
- Being helpful and cooperative
- Following up on promises and honoring commitments
- Acting natural and genuine
- Revealing something personal about yourself to show that you trust your listeners (trust needs to be a reciprocal act)
- Being sincere, truthful, and ethical in all that you say and do

- Showing that you understand important things about the listeners
- Having your actions match your words
- Having words, voice, and body language all send the same message
- Maintaining steady eye contact
- Acting poised, assured, and confident when speaking
- Acting in a consistent and predictable manner
- Demonstrating depth of knowledge concerning the subject and referring to notes only briefly
- Providing complete, current, and correct information
- Citing sources for important information
- Being willing to say "I don't know" rather than bluffing or guessing at answers to questions
- Admitting past mistakes readily
- Using facts and statistics in an objective manner without any attempt to manipulate the data or the listeners
- Quoting authorities on the subject
- Offering solid evidence to support the positions taken on various issues

Listen Reciprocally

If you listen to them you will be listened to.

—William Saroyan

To reciprocate is to have a mutual or equivalent interchange. It is to return in kind. In a communications context it means that after the person who is speaking is finished speaking, he or she then listens to what the person who has been listening has to say.

People are more inclined to listen to you and will try harder to understand what you are saying when you reciprocate by listening to them (and showing that you are doing your best to understand them—you need to listen to be heard).

It is wise not to assume that you understand anything said to you. And it is a good idea to verify anything said to you that you think you may not understand fully (when in doubt find out). It is also wise to refrain from jumping to conclusions or making premature judgments about either the person speaking or what he or she is saying.

In order to truly listen reciprocally you need a mindset that is centered more on the other person than on your own self. There are many ways you can show your listeners that you sincerely want to listen to and understand them. There are two approaches you can take to achieve this: (1) verbal and (2) nonverbal.

Let's first look at the verbal ways you can show that you either understand or are making an effort to understand what the person speaking is saying:

- Repeat, word for word, what has been said to you (mirroring).
- Repeat the essence of what was said to you in your own words (paraphrasing).
- Ask related follow-up questions about the essence of what you heard.
- Make related or corresponding comments that build upon what was said.
- Cite comparable events in your life that are connected to the speaker's remarks.
- Respond with words that contain the same level or type of feelings as the words used by the person speaking.
- Use a similar tone of voice to match the tone of the speaker's message.
- Express interest by saying "Would you tell me more about ..."
- Seek to clarify what was said by comments such as:
  1. "This is what I heard you say; do I have it right?"
  2. "I'm not sure I heard you correctly; would you run it by me again?"
- State your reactions to what was said.
- Give your reasons for agreeing or disagreeing with what you heard.
- Say reassuring things such as:
  "I understand" (with an empathetic look and voice tone)
  "I can see why you feel as you do."

"I know, I've been there too."

"I would feel the same way if I were in your place."

"I know what you mean; the same thing happened to me."

Let's now examine several nonverbal things you can do to show you are on the same wavelength and understand the person speaking:

- Look directly at the person with an attentive body posture.
- Have an interested look on your face.
- React with facial expressions that are in harmony with what is being said at the time.
- Nod your head up and down or sideways in response to what is being said.
- Make sounds that are compatible with what is being said (for example, hmm, um, oh, and ah).
- Remain silent and hear the person out without any interruptions or restless movements of your body.
- Demonstrate you can do what the speaker talked about or asked you to do.

Act Enthusiastic

Nothing great was ever achieved without enthusiasm.

—Ralph Waldo Emerson

An enthusiastic speaker displays excitement, zeal, and a strong liking for his or her subject and the opportunity to speak about it.

Enthusiasm is contagious. You need to show that you are enthusiastic about your subject if you expect your listeners to be enthusiastic about it. If your listeners are not excited about the topic and your presentation style, they will not be attentive and will consequently make little effort to understand what you are saying.

In addition to conveying enthusiasm for your subject, you need to show that you like your listeners and are excited about the opportunity to talk with them.

You can show your enthusiasm in these ways:

- Making a statement about your strong commitment to the subject
- Telling about your conviction regarding the topic in a manner that reveals how intensely you feel about the subject
- Sharing your personal experiences regarding the topic
- Demonstrating an extensive knowledge of the subject
- Having animated facial expressions while speaking
- Using frequent movement and free-flowing gestures
- Speaking with a lively and expressive voice
- Saying some things with a rising voice volume and at a faster rate of speech
- Using action language with a punch
- Interacting with your listeners in as many ways as possible
- Smiling often and showing you are enjoying yourself

Get and Maintain Attention

Attention is a hard thing to get from men.

—Francis Bacon

Attention is the readiness of the listener to hear what the person speaking is saying. Focus and concentration are synonyms for attention.

Your first step toward getting understood is gaining and maintaining your listeners' attention. No understanding can occur without adequate attention. Strive to get your listeners to concentrate exclusively on what you are saying.

The challenge of securing your listeners' attention is a constant one. This is a tremendous challenge because people are bombarded with thousands of messages daily. It is a mistake to assume that people are paying attention to what you are saying just because they are present and looking at you (people are good at faking attention). People can pay close attention to only one thing at a time. People have short attention spans. They listen in spurts and their mind wanders periodically.

To gain attention you need a strong beginning when talking with people. Your opening comments are extremely important as they are the key to getting people to focus on what you are saying. It is wise to delay your opening statement until your listeners are settled and ready to focus their attention on you. One effective way to begin is by stating your purpose. Another strong beginning is to stress how what you are going to say will benefit your listeners. Answer the question "so what?" immediately. Still another approach is to make a startling statement or to cite a powerful and relevant quotation by someone important to your listeners.

You can also create interest by establishing common ground with your listeners. Reveal something about yourself that your listeners can connect with. This helps to make what you are saying relate directly to your listeners' lives.

It also helps to establish your credibility immediately. When people know your qualifications for speaking on the topic, they will be more inclined to listen to you. A quick summary of your experience, training, and expertise on the subject shared in a modest manner will show your listeners why you are worth listening to.

Organize your remarks carefully and logically to maintain your listeners' attention. Limit the amount of information you present or you will overwhelm people and they will consequently tune you out. Your ideas should be organized in a sequence that is easy to follow. Give your main point right away and then number your other main points as you offer them. Carefully show your transitions when going from point to point. Emphasize your key points by pausing or repeating them, and be sure to summarize your main points when ending your talk.

To gain and maintain attention, present your information in an enthusiastic and lively style. Vary your speaking speed and try to speak at a rate of 125 to 150 words a minute (if you speak too fast or too slow you may lose your listeners' attention). Also, change your voice volume and use appropriate gestures to hold people's attention.

Use simple language and words that are familiar to your listeners. Use short words and sentences rather than long ones. Speak in specifics rather than in generalities. Use language that creates a mental picture and visual aids to make your comments more interesting and easy to understand.

While using visual aids, be sure to look at your listeners and ensure that the visuals are large enough to be seen easily.

Your words should sound spontaneous rather than rehearsed. Use fresh phrases that inject life and color into your language rather than employing trite and tired phrases. Provide new information and fresh ideas to create interest and maintain attention. Speak about everyday events and real-life incidents important to your listeners. Conversely, avoid talking about things people already know and that are common place.

Other things that help you to gain and hold the attention of your listeners include:

- Using impressive quotations related to the subject
- Asking rhetorical questions to involve people
- Employing humor that is in good taste and that is relevant to the point you are making

CHAPTER 2

Organization of the Message

Know and Accept Your Responsibilities as a Speaker

Responsibility is like a string that we can see only the middle of. Both ends are out of sight.

—William McFee

Responsibility is something that a person is accountable for. It is something a person is answerable for doing. It is a duty or function a person is obligated to fulfill.

When speaking, you have the primary responsibility for getting what you are saying understood by the people listening. These responsibilities are numerous and almost endless. Conversely, the people listening are only expected to make a reasonable effort to understand what is being said to them.

The major responsibilities of a speaker are detailed in the various sections of this book and include:

- Having a clear purpose and stating this upfront to the listeners
- Thinking clearly and presenting one's thoughts in an organized and logical sequence
- Making a sincere and concerted effort to get understood
- Knowing the subject thoroughly and demonstrating competence on the topic
- Learning as much about the listeners and their expectations as possible
- Establishing rapport and a sense of commonality as quickly as possible
- Creating a trusting climate
- Using clear, simple, and familiar language when speaking

- Speaking with the most effective style for the type of message, occasion, and listeners
- Providing accurate, complete, and current information in an objective, fair, and balanced manner
- Adapting the content and language to the people listening
- Sending a clear, explicit, and consistent message by means of the choice of words, voice tone, and body language
- Being enthusiastic so that the message will be interesting as well as informative
- Emphasizing, summarizing, and explaining the main points
- Being as brief as possible by limiting the information presented to only the most important and relevant ideas
- Using correct grammar and pronouncing words properly
- Timing the message for optimal results
- Balancing compassion with candor when sharing bad news or unwelcome information
- Verifying that what you are saying is getting understood by obtaining prompt feedback

It is imperative that you as the speaker not only understand these responsibilities but also carry them out to the best of your ability.

Plan and Organize the Message

A bad beginning makes a bad ending.

—Euripides

You need to organize your content if you want to be more easily understood. Organizing the content means arranging the information into a coherent unity or systematically into a logical sequence.

The first step in organizing what you want to say is to identify your purpose. You need to pin down specifically what you want to achieve with your remarks. Later, when you begin to make your comments it is wise to state your purpose right away so your listeners will know immediately what to expect from your message.

After identifying your purpose the next step is to decide on the main points you want to make. Next, organize the main points into a logical order by developing an outline. Your main points need to be connected to your purpose. Each main point should be independent of and separate from your other main points. It is best to limit the number of main points so that your listeners (and readers) will not be overwhelmed with information. By limiting the number of main points you also emphasize their importance. (Remember, when everything you say is of equal importance nothing is of special importance).

Use the outline to connect and coordinate your main points and subpoints. The outline guides the reader's thinking by providing a skeleton of the essence of your message. In addition, the outline separates your main ideas from your subordinate ideas. Your outline should be brief and contain only keywords and phrases rather than complete sentences. The logical order of your ideas should enable your listeners to make clear and easy transitions in their thinking as you proceed with your comments point to point.

After your outline is complete, write brief notes of the things you want to say to your listeners. Next, consider the best way to state the information you want to share. (Be sure to talk with your listeners rather than read to them.) Finally, practice what you want to say and how you want to say it. Practice enough to guarantee you are comfortable and familiar with your material, but beware of practicing too much or you risk your presentation sounding stale. Here are several tips that you will find helpful when determining the best order for presenting your information:

- Present your most important information at the beginning and ending of your remarks. Avoid placing them in the middle where they could be overlooked.
- Put your main ideas first followed by the supporting information.
- State simple ideas before complex concepts.
- Present known and familiar information or ideas before discussing new or unfamiliar ideas.
- Offer noncontroversial ideas your listeners will agree with before introducing less popular or controversial information.
- Try to gain instant agreement and rapport with your listeners to establish a favorable relationship.

- Try to ascertain if your listeners prefer to first hear the conclusion to your topic followed by the background information that leads to the conclusion or vice versa.
- Finish strong with well-rehearsed final comments.

Make an Effective Introduction

Well begun is half done.

—Anonymous

An introduction is a preliminary statement to the main portion of a presentation. It is your beginning or opening statement that leads into the body of your presentation.

Your introduction is tremendously important to the success of your talk because it sets the tone for the entire presentation. You need to get off to a good start because it is difficult to recover from a bad beginning.

An introduction is used to:

- Announce the topic
- State the purpose of your talk
- Create interest and gain attention
- Inform the people listening about how they will benefit from your comments
- Establish your credibility for speaking on the topic
- Build goodwill and establish areas of mutual agreement (commonality)
- Preview the main ideas you will be offering
- Provide necessary background for the body of your talk

Keep your introduction brief and simple. It is also advisable to delay choosing the content of your introduction until you have finished organizing your talk.

There are various ways you can introduce a topic, such as:

- State the title of your talk and your purpose for speaking about it.

- Explain the importance of the subject.
- State the problem or issue involved.
- Describe precisely how your listeners will benefit.
- Cite your personal interest and experience concerning the topic.
- Refer to people and events of interest to your listeners.
- Make a startling or controversial statement to grab your listeners' attention.
- Give an overview by summarizing the major points you will be covering.
- Cite a powerful quotation that is pertinent to the topic.
- Tell a relevant story or anecdote.
- Emphasize the importance of the occasion.
- Define the key technical or specialized terms that are essential for your listeners to understand your comments.
- Explain complex concepts regarding the essence of your talk.
- Ask a rhetorical question, or a series of questions, to motivate those listening.
- Tell a short, humorous story that relates to the topic.

Make an Effective Conclusion

Great is the art of beginning, but greater is the art of ending.
—Henry Wadsworth Longfellow

A conclusion is the closing part of a discourse. It is the ending, completion, or finish of a presentation.

A conclusion has two primary purposes:

1. To let your listeners know you are ending your talk
2. To refresh your listeners' memory regarding the central theme and the major ideas of your talk

People retain best what you say at the beginning and ending of your presentation. This is why it is imperative that you provide an effective conclusion. A conclusion should be brief and definite, but it should not be sudden or abrupt. It should leave no doubt that you have finished your talk. It is also a good idea to end on a positive and upbeat note.

As is true for the introduction, there are several effective ways you can wrap up your talk. These include:

- Summarizing and reinforcing your main ideas
- Restating the importance or purpose of your talk
- Reviewing how the listeners can benefit from what you've said
- Citing a dramatic quotation related to your subject
- Issuing a challenge or call to action
- Making an emotional appeal
- Asking a provocative question for the listeners to ponder
- Predicting future events based on the facts you presented
- Proposing a specific plan of action
- Telling your listeners where they can obtain more information
- Announcing the beginning of the question-and-answer period and how it will be conducted

CHAPTER 3

Content of the Message

The Eight-C's Octagon of an Effective Communication

Essential communications skills for managers: A practical guide for communicating effectively with all people in all situations

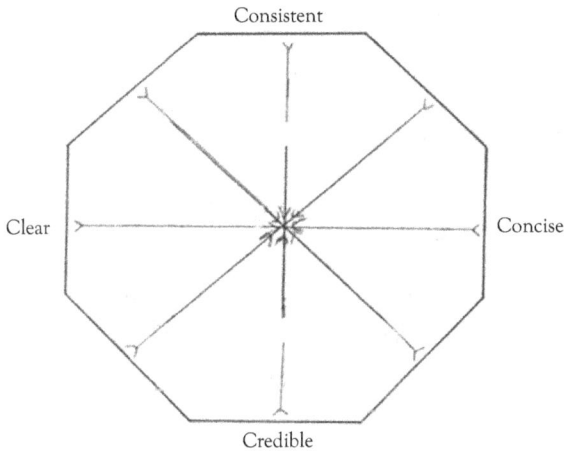

Consistent

Clear

Concise

Credible

Create and Maintain People's Interest

Talk in terms of your listeners' interests

—Dale Carnegie

Interest is having a feeling of curiosity, attentiveness, or concern about something. The words attention and interest are so closely related that they are often used interchangeably.

People have always faced the challenges of gaining and holding the interest of their listeners. It is presumptuous to assume that just because you are interested in your topic, your listeners are also interested—it just ain't so.

You need to motivate your listeners or they won't listen to you. To motivate them you need to make them feel that their needs and wants will be satisfied by the information you are sharing. Therefore, it is important for you to show immediately how your message will benefit your listeners. You need to answer "so what?" for people to get their attention and keep it.

There are many things you can do to get and keep your listeners' interest. These include:

- Start with a startling statement that shocks your listeners.
- State a dramatic statistic or an impressive quotation connected to your topic.
- Demonstrate your strong interest in both your topic and your listeners themselves.
- Explain clearly and specifically why you consider the topic to be so important along with your experience concerning the topic.
- Refer to people and events that are known to your listeners (for example, local people, events, and problems).
- Personalize your message and try to involve your listeners as much as you can.
- Present new and unusual facts related to your topic.
- State a controversial opinion.
- Tell a brief story of special interest to the people.
- Ask a provocative question and then pause briefly to give people time to mull the question over.
- Relate a humorous incident that is related to something happening at the time.
- Speak in a lively, enthusiastic manner (vary your voice volume, tone, and pitch).
- Talk at a brisk rate and in a confident manner.
- Speak fluently and smoothly without any awkward pauses.
- Be listener centered by saying "you" and "we" frequently and avoiding the words "I," "me," and "my" as much as possible.
- Use fresh words and lively phrases (avoid tired, overused, boring ways of saying things).
- Use picture-words that create a mental image in your listeners' mind.

- Say things in different ways to avoid sounding repetitive and monotonous.
- Try to minimize any distractions that compete for your listeners' attention.

Adapt the Content

What we anticipate seldom occurs: what we least expect generally happens

—Benjamin Disraeli

When we adapt our message we adjust it, modify it, and fit it to the particular situation and nature of our listeners.

Since being flexible is basic to getting yourself understood, your ongoing goal should be to be sufficiently flexible so that you can customize your approach as needed. It is important to realize that an approach that aids getting understood by one person may not promote understanding by someone else.

To adapt your message content, wording, and speaking style you need to know your listeners and the situation at the time. In order to truly know someone else you need to be other person centered and less self-centered. Frequent use of the word "you" makes you seem more other person centered whereas the frequent use of "I" and "me" makes you appear to be more self-centered.

Show your listeners you care for them by doing your best to learn what is important to them, their interests, goals, ambitions, beliefs, needs, blind spots, and touchy areas. After learning these things about your listeners, adapt your message content, word choices, and speaking style based on what you have learned.

Your comments should focus on what is important and interesting to your listeners, or your message will be less understood or may even be tuned out.

Examples of how to adjust your message to your listeners include:

- If they prefer the conclusions before getting background information, use this sequence when presenting information and vice versa.

- If they want to draw their own conclusions from the data you provide then don't state the conclusions.
- Use examples and explanations that are related to your listeners' experiences and backgrounds.
- If they like details and plenty of examples and anecdotes, present them.
- Select a setting preferred by your listeners (e.g., formal or informal).
- Choose the best day and time of day for your listeners.
- Adapt the type of content to the knowledge and backgrounds of your listeners.
- Use a vocabulary level consistent with the educational level of your listeners as well as words that are familiar to them.
- Use a presentation style based on your listeners' preferences.
- Include a cross section of your listeners when planning your presentation.
- Observe the facial expressions and body language of your listeners as you speak, and make adjustments based on this feedback.

Provide Complete Information

Experience is never limited and is never complete

—Henry James

A complete message contains all the necessary and important information about something—nothing essential is left out. A complete message is thorough. It is whole rather than partial. A whole message should answer the five Ws and one H: who, what, where, when, why, and how.

Your goal is to provide your listeners all the information they need without overwhelming them with too much information at one time. Supply complete information with sufficient details in as few words as possible. You need to offer all significant details to get understood, but not every detail.

When you send only partial messages, you create confusion, misunderstanding, and even mistrust. When crucial information is left out, your listeners will sense that something is missing and wonder what you've omitted and why. Partial messages can cause problems. When incomplete information is shared the message becomes suspect. And in turn, the sender may lose credibility and the trust of his or her listeners. Additionally, the resulting misunderstanding can result in time and money being wasted.

Identify the essential and nonessential information when preparing your message. Ask yourself, "What information is necessary for my listeners to know in order for them to understand what I am saying?"

Begin the preparation of your message by gathering all the data related to your subject. Next, sort the information and decide which information is essential and which is not. Then, develop your outline listing all of your main points and the subpoints that support your main ideas. Next, revise your outline based on your purpose, nature of the subject, and speaking time available. Then, practice your delivery aloud to determine how your ideas connect and whether the content sounds complete and organized to your own ears. The final step is to revise your content based on this assessment.

In the final analysis, completeness is measured by how adequate your listeners consider the information you've provided.

Offer Relevant Information

You learn easier and remember better that which is interesting and relevant to your life

—Joseph DeVito

When something is relevant to a person, it is important and significant to him or her. It is pertinent, germane, and closely related to the matter being discussed.

To achieve your purpose when speaking, you need to gather and present ideas and information that are relevant to your purpose. Conversely, omit any ideas and information that are not pertinent to your goal for speaking.

When presenting it is helpful to ask yourself these questions periodically:

1. Is what I am saying now directly related to my purpose for speaking?
2. Is what I am saying really significant?
3. Does what I am saying really contribute anything or make a difference?

    If the answer to any of these questions is no, do not include the material in your talk.

Relevancy of content has two dimensions:

- It must be relevant in your opinion.
- It must be viewed as relevant by the people listening to you.

Realize that a speaker can be interesting, eloquent, and enthusiastic and yet say nothing worth listening to. Remember, to promote understanding a speaker needs to talk less and say more.

Limit the Amount of Information

Knowledge is of two kinds. We know a subject ourselves or we know where we can find it

—Samuel Johnson

You limit the information presented to your listeners by restricting the quantity or amount of material you offer to them at any one time.

It is vital that you realize that people can absorb only a limited amount of information at one time. Brief messages are not only easier to absorb but emphasize your main points.

The amount of data your listeners can digest depends on three things:

1. The complexity of the subject matter
2. People's familiarity with the content
3. Their capacity to grasp what you are saying (People don't want to work hard to figure out what you are saying).

Your goal should be to provide quality not quantity of information. You can limit the information shared if you:

- Ask yourself before you say anything, "What does what I am about to say have to do with my purpose and how important is it?"
- Relate all information directly to your purpose
- Stay on track and on target with every comment
- Say only what needs to be said then stop
- Keep your words and sentences short
- Eliminate all irrelevant information even though it may be interesting and entertaining, and thus save time
- Spread out important information and offer it in bite-size chunks
- Select only information that is compatible with your listeners' level of knowledge and sophistication
- Take time to get feedback from your listeners on every important point before moving on to the next point

Make Concrete Statements

Prefer the specific to the general, the definite to the vague and the concrete to the abstract

William Strunk and E.B. White

Concrete words refer to specific objects, events, people, material, places, and things. They are real and tangible. They can be experienced by the senses (they can be seen—the state of liberty, they can be heard—symphonic music, they can be touched—a woolen sweater, and they can be smelled—cabbage cooking). A concrete word is the opposite of an abstract word.

Concrete words put otherwise difficult concepts into terms that are familiar and real to people. Tangible words stir up mental associations and stimulate your listeners' recalling certain experiences.

The use of some abstract statements is inevitable. However, they should be used only when necessary. Abstract words are often meaningless because they are fuzzy and lie outside the experiences of the people listening. Abstractions frequently deal with such intangibles as peoples' feelings, values, and beliefs.

The more abstract the word the more difficult it is to understand. Here are a few examples showing the more ambiguous an abstraction becomes, the more difficult it is to understand.

Concrete words:	dollar bill	tomato	catcher
Less concrete words:	money	vegetable	baseball player
Abstract words:	value	nutrition	athlete

You can make your comments more concrete and less abstract by doing the following:

- Before using an abstract word, narrow down the concept and find a more concrete term to substitute for it. For example, say Cadillac for luxury car, penicillin for miracle drug, and collie instead of family pet.
- Describe the specifics of an actual thing or event—for example, a car accident, graduation ceremony, or football game.
- Provide relevant facts and statistics about something. For example, say 1.3 trillion dollars instead of massive spending, 700 people killed rather than widespread loss of life, or 40 years old instead of middle aged.
- Use familiar examples related to the lives of your listeners that create mental images (pictures) in their minds (e.g., a rustic, rambling farmhouse surrounded by high grass and birch trees instead of only farmhouse).

Provide Accurate Information

Some degree of accuracy must be sacrificed to conciseness
—Samuel Johnson

An accurate message is correct, truthful, and free from error. Accurate information is objective, balanced, and factual. In addition, it is valid, reliable, and complete. In order to be understood you need to use words both accurately and correctly.

It is important to recognize the effect of the accuracy of your message on your credibility and on how your message is understood. It is also important to be aware of the favorable and unfavorable feelings that certain words and information can arouse in your listeners, because these feelings can influence the accuracy of your listeners' interpretation of what you are saying. The correctness of your information can be no better than the related facts you have gathered on the topic.

To avoid sharing inaccurate information you need to avoid hit-and-miss or slated ways of gathering information. A recommended approach is as follows:

1. Collect all the pertinent information on the topic.
2. Verify the correctness, timeliness, and completeness of the data you collect.
3. Separate the facts gathered from opinions, beliefs, and inferences.
4. Discard all but the factual data.
5. Analyze the facts to get them straight (understood) in your own mind.
6. Use only the best of the remaining information.

It is essential that you ask yourself whether the information you are going to convey is based on facts, inferences, opinions, or value judgments. Here is an example to help you to differentiate among these factors.

- Fact: The car is black. Black cars get hot because they draw more heat from the sun.
- Opinion: White cars are better than black cars.
- Value judgment: I don't like to be hot so I don't like black cars.
- Inference: Since black cars are hot, all cars irrespective of color are hot.

In the event that you give out some incorrect information or sense it has been misunderstood, immediately try to remedy the situation by saying something like this, "Sorry, hold on, what I said did not come out right; let me state it in a different way."

Remember when talking with people that your constant goal is to share accurate information at all times.

Send a Consistent Message

A foolish consistency is the hobgoblin of little minds
—Ralph Waldo Emerson

A consistent message is marked by harmony, coherence, and compatibility. All parts of the message hang together in a unified manner. There is an absence of conflicting and contradictory information.

Your verbal and nonverbal messages need to be consistent, or misunderstanding will result. Whenever your words and body language are inconsistent, you send mixed messages to your listeners (when this happens most people believe that your body language is conveying the true message).

These tips should help you to send consistent messages:

- Be sure of what your words and body language are communicating to people.
- Make sure that your words and body language (facial expressions, posture, gestures, and movement) agree with each other and are transmitting the same message.
- Have your appearance and language be consistent with and appropriate for the occasion, subject matter, and listeners' expectations.
- Be certain that your content and style of delivery are complementary. For example, a serious topic requires a serious, business-like presentation style.
- Convey information that is clear and noncontradictory. The points you are presenting need to agree with each other and be mutually supportive of your overall goal.
- Use grammar that is proper and consistent. For example, (1) subject and verb should agree, (2) nouns and pronouns need to agree, and (3) your tenses should agree.

- Strive to have your words, voice tone, voice volume, rate of speaking, facial expressions, and body language all say the same thing at the same time.

The best way to develop trust and thus promote understanding is to be consistent in what you are saying and how you are saying it.

CHAPTER 4

Context of a Message

Consider the Context Carefully

In addition to analyzing specific listeners, you will have to devote some attention to the specific context in which you speak.

—Joseph DeVito

Context is the weaving together of words or parts of a discussion that surround a word or passage that can throw light on its meaning. Context is also the interrelated conditions in which your speaking occurs.

Context includes such factors as:

people involved	timing	preceding and following events
communications climate	location	distracting noise and activity
the situation	the occasion	seating arrangement
related information	listeners	expectations of listeners
previous knowledge		

Context is tremendously important in giving meaning to words. It determines the sense in which a word is used and interpreted. The full meaning of a word can't be understood until it is placed in a certain context. The same word can mean different things to different people in different situations. Here are several examples to illustrate how the meaning of words varies depending on their context:

- A woman seductively whispers "I hate you" into the ear of her lover as they cuddle.
- A New Englander says "It is snowing" to an Eskimo and receives a blank stare because Eskimos have many words that are used to show gradients for different kinds of snow. Consequently, one word for snow doesn't really communicate anything to them.

- A watchmaker views one inch as a large measurement whereas a bulldozer operator perceives one inch as being miniscule.
- A person from Florida may comment "It sure is cold today" while a resident of Maine may remark "It is rather warm today" when they are at the same place and the temperature is 50 degrees.
- The word "soon" often means something different to a Hispanic person than it does to a person with Anglo-Saxon heritage because of the difference in their cultures.

It is also worth noting that the same word can have many meanings. For example, the word "set" has over two hundred meanings and can have different meanings in different contexts: a set of China; set the flowers over there; he won in the final set of tennis. The words "run" and "cat" also have many different meanings.

Understanding is frequently affected by the feelings that certain words evoke; for example:

- The word "union" is viewed favorably by factory workers and with disdain by many people with management positions.
- The word "police" is perceived differently by people living in a dictatorship than it is by those living in a democracy.
- The word "liberal" is viewed differently by Democrats than by Republicans.
- The word "hunger" has a different meaning to the people in Haiti than it does to most Americans.

These examples demonstrate how strongly context influences meaning and emphasizes the need to consider context when you are talking about important matters. It is imperative that you consider the many contexts of a word if you want to get your message understood.

Understand Your Listeners' Culture

The greatest law of culture: let each become all that he was created capable of being.

—Thomas Carlyle

A culture is the customary beliefs, social forms, and material traits of a racial, ethnic, religious, or particular group of people. Our culture tells us what to believe as well as how to think and act.

In order to communicate effectively you need to understand and appreciate cultural diversity. You need to adapt your communications, attitudes, style, and language to your listeners' culture. It would be naive to expect that members of different cultures will interpret what they hear in the same way. It would be equally naive to expect that an acceptable way of communicating in one culture would also be acceptable in another culture. Each of us has his or her own unique culture. No two cultures are alike. However, some are more similar and dissimilar than others.

The cultural differences of your listeners are important for you to be aware of when you are organizing and delivering a talk, whether to a group or a single individual. Important cultural differences that can cause misunderstanding include:

gender	religious	educational level
age	social class	type of occupation
racial	regional	nationality
ethnic	spoken language	political affiliations

Let's look at several examples of how cultural differences affect communication and getting understood:

1. Gender
   Men and women communicate differently. Men tend to dominate conversations and to interrupt more often than women. Men usually say things in a more direct and frank manner and let the chips fall where they may, whereas women tend to be more sensitive and talk more about their feelings. In addition, women generally state things more indirectly and delicately.

2. Ethnic and Racial
   People of different racial and ethnic backgrounds vary in how direct or indirect they are in their speech, the formality or informality of their style of speaking, how they express agreement and disagreement, and their use of body language (e.g., Japanese-Americans).

3. Religious

Some religions impact more deeply on people's daily lives. Some emphasize the past, some the present, and others the future to a greater extent. Religions often define the roles of family members differently (e.g., Muslims-Christians).

4. Regional

Traditions, customs, and lifestyle vary in different regions of a country. Some use standard American speech and pronunciation whereas others have unique dialects and use frequent colloquialisms when speaking. The types of occupations and political and religious beliefs also may vary considerably (e.g., the Deep South-New England).

5. Language Use

People prefer to speak in their own language, to say and hear words that they are familiar and comfortable with. It is important to realize that words in one language do not always have an equivalent meaning in another language. In fact, the meaning of words can differ even within the same country.

6. Voice

Speaking with a loud voice is acceptable in some cultures and resented in others. A friendly, informal speaking style may be viewed as appropriate in some cultures and inappropriate and rude in others (e.g., British-Americans).

7. Body Language

Frequent and steady eye contact is viewed favorably in certain cultures and unfavorably in others. The meaning of various body movements and gestures is also interpreted differently. For example, in some cultures nodding the head up and down means no, while in others it means yes. Perfectly innocent gestures by people in one culture may be perceived as obscene and rude in others. For example, showing the soles of your shoes to the person you are conversing with is an extreme insult in Japan.

8. Space

Standing or sitting close to another person while speaking is considered comfortable and desirable by people in some cultures. Conversely, people from other cultures find such closeness to be objectionable and distasteful. For instance, people from countries nearer to the equator tend to prefer closer proximity than those located farther from the equator.

9. Time

Various cultures perceive time differently. For example, some emphasize the future and project a sense of urgency when communicating, while others focus on the past with no sense of immediacy. For example, people with a northern European background typically reflect more urgency than do people with a Hispanic heritage.

10. Colors and Numbers

Even numbers and colors can cause communications problems. In some cultures certain numbers and colors are associated with either good or bad luck. However, in other cultures these are not important factors to consider when communicating. For example, the number 7 is considered lucky and the number 13 unlucky by some Americans, whereas those from other cultures see other numbers as having special significance.

You can improve your chances of getting understood by people from different cultures by doing the following:

- Observe how the members of various cultures communicate with each other   especially their use of body language.
- Learn the cultural backgrounds of your listeners and adapt your content, organization, and delivery accordingly.
- Show that you accept and understand the particular culture of your listeners; however, be careful not to stereotype any group of people.
- Pronounce names and places that relate to other cultures correctly.
- Be patient and diplomatic when speaking and listening— don't show frustration or irritation when what you are saying doesn't appear to be getting across.
- Speak slowly, distinctly, and loudly enough to be easily understood. Avoid merely talking louder or just repeating the same words in an effort to get understood better.
- Use simple words that are familiar to your listeners (refrain from using slang, idioms, acronyms, and technical terms).

- Limit sentences to one idea and use short words and sentences when saying something.
- Be as clear and explicit as possible (avoid implications and subtlety).
- Match the rate of your speaking to the type of content and the backgrounds of your listeners.
- Emphasize and summarize key information.
- Cite examples frequently.
- Use words that create mental images for people (showing visuals will help you to do this).
- Be sure your facial expressions, gestures, and body movements are appropriate and don't offend people.
- Obtain frequent feedback by watching body language and asking questions.

Provide Sufficient Time

There is a right time and a wrong time to say and do everything.
—Walter St. John

Time is a measurable period of duration during which an action, process, or condition exists or continues. The goal is to allocate adequate time to get what you want to say said clearly and understood.

Select the best time, for both yourself and your listeners, to discuss an important matter or to share bad news (some examples are subsequently discussed).

It is essential that you organize your time. The importance of a topic and the amount of content together determine the time needed to discuss the subject sufficiently. The opposite is also true: The time available limits the amount of information that you can convey at one time. Therefore, the time available and the amount of information you want to present need to be properly balanced.

Give important information more time and unimportant information less time. You need to allocate more time to the important content in order to emphasize and clarify it. The time devoted to each main topic depends on the amount and complexity of the supporting information for each. Allocate sufficient time to each main topic but be careful not to provide an excessive amount of time for any one topic.

It is a mistake to offer too much information in too little time. Be discriminating and limit the amount of information to be shared according to the time available.

Generally, a presentation should not exceed one hour. It is a good idea to limit your speaking to a maximum of 40 minutes and the question-and-answer (Q and A) period to 20 minutes (most listeners' attention begins to fade after 20 minutes or so).

Start preparing early for a presentation to a group (preferably one to two weeks before). Allow yourself plenty of time to collect, screen, and organize your data, as well as to practice your talk. It is a good idea to organize your data in a chronological order that follows the sequence of events as they occurred.

Respect and honor the time limits for your presentation. Start on time and end on time! Begin with a short introduction, and speak at a rate of 120 to 150 words a minute. State key information more slowly than less important information (stop promptly when finished—don't drag it out).

Time your presentation when practicing (be sure to practice aloud). Time not only your total presentation but each of the major topics separately so that you can analyze your time allocations and adjust them as needed (it helps to use a watch or clock with a second hand).

Keep continuous track of the time while making your presentation. Time has a way of getting away from speakers before they know it. Place your watch and a card with the ending time on the lectern where you can see them easily and frequently. By checking your watch or a clock periodically you can be fully aware of how you are doing time-wise (don't just guess about the time remaining).

You want to avoid the pitfall of suddenly realizing that your time is almost up and that you still have several important things to say. Also, avoid the temptation to speed up the end of your presentation and thus cause your listeners to feel rushed and overwhelmed.

These tips should enable you to make efficient use of time:

- Determine the exact purpose of your presentation. Take time to consider the key things you want to say and how to best say them.
- Learn crucial facts about your listeners.
- Pilot-test your talk with people representative of the group you will be addressing. Revise the content based on this feedback.
- Predict the possible reactions to your remarks so that you can deal with them proactively.
- Build rapport and establish your credibility at the beginning of your remarks (be brief).
- Select the best wording to get your ideas across before you say anything of consequence.
- Consider how much time people need to absorb what you have told them—pause accordingly.
- Get ongoing feedback to clarify any misunderstandings (seek it immediately when people look confused).
- Pause to emphasize key points.
- Repeat important ideas several times to reinforce them.
- Show clear transition when you go from one idea to the next.
- Respond to questions during your talk at appropriate times (usually immediately after you have completed conveying your thought).
- Repeat all of the questions asked thus far during the Q and A period.
- When asked a question during Q and A, pause briefly to make sure you understand the question and to give yourself time to consider your answer.

You can save time by doing the following:

- Define and narrow the purpose of your presentation.
- Identify and limit the number of major topics and the supporting information for each.

- Provide sufficient advance notice to people regarding the time, place, and topic.
- Send necessary background information a few days ahead of time so people can become more knowledgeable and better prepared.
- Cut out any unnecessary information and words that add nothing to the discourse.
- Eliminate time-wasting sounds such as uh, er, um. Avoid ending sentences with "okay" and eliminate empty phrases such as "you know" and other similar phrases.
- Avoid making rambling comments and irrelevant remarks.
- Use unrelated humor sparingly; for example, telling long, involved jokes.
- Remain standing while conversing with individuals and small groups.
- Use visuals only when they clarify information, and offer them in a concise manner.

It is worth noting that you can often say more with fewer words thus guaranteeing that you have sufficient time for your presentation.

CHAPTER 5

Word and Language Use

Develop an Extensive Vocabulary

Tis what I feel, but can't define, tis what I know, but can't express.
—Beilby Porteus

A person's vocabulary is the sum and variety of words he or she has available to use when speaking or writing.

The bigger your vocabulary, the better. By having an extensive vocabulary you are able to choose the exact words that best say what you want to say about something. The use of precise language is required for a person to get understood optimally.

Generally, use short, simple words and plain, easy-to-understand language rather than long words and fancy language. However, it is permissible to use long words when they most precisely express what you are thinking and feeling. The fact is that sometimes there are no satisfactory substitute or alternate words to select from—for example, when speaking about specialized fields such as science and medicine.

Standard or commonly used words generally communicate best. Your listeners must be able to understand the words you use or there will be a communications breakdown. Therefore, refrain from using slang, idioms, and foreign words, as well as long, unfamiliar words and phrases.

The backgrounds, educational level, and intellectual abilities of your listeners limit the level of vocabulary you can use. If you use high-level vocabulary, your uneducated listeners won't understand you. Conversely, if you use low-level vocabulary, you are likely to offend your educated listeners. In these instances you will be either talking over the heads of people or talking down to them. In either case, you risk being misunderstood and may even antagonize people.

Use words familiar to your listeners. Also, be sure that the words you use have the same basic meaning for both you and your listeners. Beware of assuming you are being understood as this is naive. If you are uncertain about whether your words are being understood, define them.

To use words correctly, you need to know precisely what they mean. If you have any doubts about the meaning of words, get into the habit of looking them up in a reputable and up-to-date dictionary. Dictionaries list words and phrases compiled from a survey of many sources. Unabridged dictionaries contain over five hundred thousand entries whereas the average adult knows only about ten thousand words. Be sure to check that the dictionary you are consulting is current as dictionary listings are always influx with words being added and deleted as times change.

In addition to using a good abridged dictionary, you would profit from using a thesaurus, or dictionary of synonyms. These aids contain words having the same or similar meanings to the word you are looking up. Your vocabulary says a lot about you. An extensive vocabulary properly employed impresses people and creates a favorable image.

You are capable of building your vocabulary if you really want to by making a reasonable effort to do so. The following tips will help you to increase your vocabulary:

- Develop an attitude of intellectual inquiry (have an urge to know and grow).
- Read widely on a variety of subjects or look up new words as you encounter them.
- Listen to what people say and analyze the context in which they used a word to figure out its meaning. If you can't determine the meaning, ask the person who used it to define it for you (even presidents have been known to interrupt a speaker to ask the person to explain what a word they said meant).
- Write down a new word soon after you hear it so you can remember it. Next, look up the new word. Notice how it is spelled and pronounced as well as what it means.
- Add the new word to your vocabulary by practicing using it frequently in sentences (both verbally and in writing).
- Feel the sense of accomplishment from having expanded your vocabulary.

Use the Best Words

The important thing about any word is how you understand it.
—Publilius Syrus

A word is a speech sound, or series of sounds, that communicates meaning. Words are symbols that stand for an idea, event, or object. Words are not the same as the idea, event, or object itself. Words are not real things and should not be confused with reality.

You have the freedom to choose what you want to say and how you want to say it. The test for whether to use a word or note is to ask yourself this question: Does the word fill a real need? If it does, use it; if it doesn't, don't use it.

Your constant goal should be to select just the right word for getting your message across as clearly as possible. Even a slight difference in words can make a tremendous difference in their interpretation. Mark Twain once made this perceptive observation about word differences: "The difference between the right word and the almost right word is the difference between lightning and the lightning bug."

There are no right words for all situations. Selecting the exact right word to describe your thoughts and feelings is not easy; in fact, it can be extremely hard. The choice is easier to make when you possess an extensive vocabulary that allows you to pick the word that contains the fine shade of meaning that you want to convey.

This statement about language use makes an astute though humorous point: "Some people use language like underwear—merely to cover the subject with anything, while others use language like lingerie to show the subject off at its best."

Your attitude about life, people, and yourself strongly influences your choice of words. The following suggestions will assist you to make the right word choices:

- Be other person centered rather than self-centered.
- Recognize that words are only words and not reality and that they have only the meaning people give them (e.g., "Sticks and stones may break my bones but words will never hurt me").

- Be willing to work hard to choose only the best words to express yourself.
- Desire to be candid and forthright.
- Choose to use simple words and plain language.
- Be willing to learn important information about your listeners so you can learn which words are best to use with them.
- Predict the ways your words could be understood so you can try to avoid using the wrong words.

These tips on word use should be helpful:

- Be aware that words and language are constantly changing.
- Know the regional differences in word use. For example, hot cakes, pancakes, and johnnycakes are all similar.
- Use few words rather than many words to say things.
- Use short words and sentences as a rule.
- Use simple words and familiar language.
- Use active instead of passive words.
- Say things in a positive rather than negative way.
- Be explicit and precise.
- Use picture words; for example, brave as a lion, thundering waterfall.
- State things in a concrete or tangible rather than in an abstract manner.
- Use gender-neutral words.
- Select words that are lively and contain punch.
- Use specific rather than vague words and avoid generalities.
- Use clear and definite words maximally and minimize the use of ambiguous words.
- Expect to be misunderstood at times so that you will be ready to explain and clarify what you've said.

Be Cautions About Word Meanings

When I use a word it means just what I choose it to mean, nothing more or less.

—Humpty Dumpty

Meaning is the sense of something that is conveyed by language. It is that which is signified by words. Meaning is what a speaker intends for a listener to understand from what is said and it is what a listener understands from what a speaker says.

The meaning of a word depends on the person saying it and the person hearing it, along with the context in which the word is used. For example, the word "holocaust" has a special meaning to a Jewish survivor of the concentration camps. The word "rape" has a unique meaning to a rape survivor. The meaning of heart attack has a much more intense personal meaning for a person who has suffered one. A word means only what the person saying it intends for it to mean at the certain time and under the particular circumstances, though the audience may not perceive the same meaning. There never has been nor will there ever be one right or absolute meaning to a word.

People give similar meaning to words only to the extent they have similar experiences. Therefore, since no two people have ever had exactly the same experiences, they cannot possibly derive exactly the same meaning for a word they say or hear. It is helpful to view words as a map of a territory and not the actual territory itself. Like a map, words are only an approximation of what they represent.

It is impossible to predict accurately the affect a word will have in any given situation since the same word can evoke positive, neutral, and negative reactions from different people; for example, the words "conservative" and "liberal."

To minimize confusion over words, constantly ask yourself when speaking, "What do I really want to say and how can I say it best?" Conversely, when listening, ask yourself, "What did the speaker mean when he or she said so-and-so?" Both speakers and listeners need to be sensitive to the many shades and subtleties of word use. It is best not to react to a word you hear until you are sure of the speaker's intended meaning. For example, what does a person mean who says, "I'm anxious to go to the Super Bowl game"? Is the speaker worried or eager about going? Or, what does a woman mean when she says, "Let's do lunch soon"? Does she sincerely want to have lunch with you or is she merely saying this to be polite without any intent to follow up and have lunch together?

Let's look at some causes of words being misunderstood:

- Sloppy, imprecise use of language; for example, "as soon as possible," "you know," or "and stuff like that."
- Changing meaning of words based on the changes in the words themselves or in the people speaking and listening differing experiences in life. For example, the word "gay" used to mean a happy state of mind and had nothing to do with sexuality. And the word "partner" was once used in referring to a business relationship, whereas today it could refer to a person who is cohabiting. Remember, meaning does not have a permanently fixed meaning.
- Ambiguity caused by the multiple meanings of words (rarely does a word have only one meaning). For example, the word cat has dozens of meanings as does the word run. How can a person know how the speaker is using a word until the context is known? For example, a person who is having a late supper may state, "I'm starving." Compare this with a person who has just been rescued from being lost in the woods without any food for a week saying, "I'm starving." The word starving is the same but the meaning is vastly different.
- Confusion resulting from a word that is pronounced the same way but that has a different meaning; for example, "The red book on the shelf is interesting" compared with the statement "I read the book on the shelf."
- A person's mood or feelings at the time influences how he or she interprets a word. For example, a man may say "I hate you" in anger to his wife and yet when he whispers "I hate you" in her ear during a romantic moment the word has an entirely different meaning. Or, a woman who is feeling depressed and meets a friend who compliments her by saying "You certainly look nice today" may later reflect on this comment and ask herself, "I wonder what she meant by that? Doesn't she think I look nice on other days?"

People speaking and listening would both profit from wearing this sign continuously in their mind: Danger, words at work.

State Ideas Clearly

I see one rule: to be clear. If I am not clear, all my world crumbles to nothing.

—Henri Stendhal

To be clear is to be easily understood. A clear message is free of ambiguity, haziness, and obscurity. Clarity creates no doubts or uncertainty. You have been clear when your listeners understand the thoughts and feelings you have expressed in essentially the same way you intended them to be understood.

Regrettably, there is often a significant difference between what the person speaking intends to say and what he or she actually says and also between what is said and what is actually heard.

It is essential to say things clearly. You can't compromise on clarity if you want to get understood. It is the speaker's responsibility to say things clearly. Don't expect your listeners to struggle to decipher what you are really trying to tell them; they can't and won't do this. People can only react to what you say not what you intended to say.

Your goal when speaking is to have your listeners understand your words exactly as you intended them to be understood. Cicero hit the nail on the head when he stated, "The aim of speaking is not simply to be understood, but to make it impossible to be misunderstood."

You can employ a multitude of methods to be clear and thus understood:

- Realize that clear expression begins with clear thinking. It is vital that you identify your purpose and keep it constantly in mind. Know exactly what you want to say and how you want to say it (always think before you speak).
- Relate everything you say to your purpose.
- Organize your ideas in an orderly and logical sequence.
- Provide complete and consistent information, including sufficient background material.
- Speak loudly enough to be heard easily. Speak at a brisk pace of 120 to 150 words a minute. Pause at appropriate times to allow your listeners time to think about what you have said.

- Pronounce your words carefully and correctly. It is best to use standard American English as your guide.
- Articulate your sounds carefully and properly.
- Give your listeners a chance to ask questions while you are speaking to secure feedback and also so that you can clarify unclear points on the spot (let people know when you begin speaking that it is okay to interrupt with questions at any time).
- Adjust your speaking style and content based on the feedback you get from your listeners.
- Use body language to support and reinforce what you are saying.
- Know these important things about word use:
  1. The use of words is very personal. Words have different meanings to different people in different contexts. Humpty Dumpty made this point crystal clear when he stated, "When I use a word it means what I choose it to mean, neither more or less."
  2. Use words precisely to aid clarity. Be sure to define how you are using words, especially when they have a special meaning or are highly technical.
  3. Use words that are familiar to your listeners as well as words that are connected to their experience. Refrain from using foreign words and unfamiliar acronyms.
  4. Use concrete or tangible words related to your listeners' lives.
  5. Use specific words and phrases rather than talking in generalities.
  6. State things as briefly, plainly, and simply as possible (and limit the amount of information you present at any one time) and use abbreviations only when they are well known.
  7. Cite relevant examples and tell stories to help explain complicated ideas. Comparisons and contrasts are also helpful when explaining complex and unfamiliar information.
  8. Develop an extensive vocabulary so you can select the best and most precise word to use to make a point more clearly.
  9. Use correct English. Be sure to have your verb tenses agree. Be certain to make your antecedents obvious when you use pronouns. In addition, have your subjects and verbs agree in form.

- Repeat important points several times to reinforce them. For example, tell people what you are going to tell them, tell them, and then tell them what you have told them.
- Make clear transitions to help people know when you are leaving one point and proceeding to the next (numbering your points is an effective way to show transitions).
- Help your listeners visualize the objects or events you are talking about by using lively and picturesque language that conjures up word pictures (e.g., little red schoolhouse). Visual aids also create mental images to support your words.
- Appeal to both sides of your listeners' brains. Appeal to the left side to have them apply logic, sequence, and order to what you are saying. Appeal to the right side of their brains to help them see the total picture and the spatial or artistic dimensions of your presentation.
- Avoid frequent use of the following confusing kinds of words and phrases because they disguise what you really mean or overly soften what you really intend to convey:
  1. Euphemisms—for example, saying pleasantly plump for fat, passed on for died, misspoke for lied, and so on
  2. Political correctness—for example, love child for bastard, disadvantaged for poor, and physically challenged for physically handicapped
  3. Doublespeak—for example, open secret, deliberate speed, bitter sweet, negative growth, working vacation

Use Simple Words

Simplify, simplify, simplify.

—Henry David Thoreau

Saying something simply is saying it by using plain words and uncomplicated language. Simple speaking avoids the use of fancy words, pinpoints the key ideas, and gets straight to the heart of the matter.

There is real power in speaking simply. Important ideas do not have to be expressed in a complicated manner. People who really know what they are talking about can say things clearly and simply. They use words only to express themselves rather than to impress people (truly "big" people use "little" words).

If there are several ways of saying the same thing, elect to say it in the simplest way. The use of simple language doesn't reflect a simple mind, and simplicity does not mean that your language must be simplistic and sound as though you are talking down to people.

Two other points need to be stressed:

1. Use of overly simple language can insult and turn off your listeners.
2. Big words are not always objectionable. They are okay if the subject requires their use (for example, something highly technical). They are also right to use if they sound natural for the speaker and are appropriate for the particular listeners.

These suggestions will assist you in speaking simply:

- Use short words, short sentences, and short paragraphs (beware of using four- and five-syllable words).
- Adapt your language to your listeners; use words only if they are suitable for your listeners.
- Use concrete and tangible words as much as you can (avoid abstractions as much as possible).
- Define all important words and phrases that are not crystal clear.
- Avoid using foreign words and phrases.
- Refrain from employing specialized and technical terms, jargon, slang, and colloquialisms.
- Speak concisely; cut out any unnecessary words.
- Limit the amount of information you share at any one time, especially if it is new and complicated.

The following quotations speak plainly, powerfully, and succinctly about the beauty of simplicity:

1. Henry Wadsworth Longfellow
   "In character, manner in all things the supreme excellence is simplicity."

2. Abraham Lincoln

   "Speak so that the most lowly can understand, and the rest will have no difficulty."

3. Ralph Waldo Emerson

   "An orator or writer is never successful until he has learned to make his words smaller than his ideas."

A speaker would be well advised to keep these quotations in mind when choosing the best way to say things to people.

Use Precise Words

When you say something, make sure you have said it.
                                        —William Strunk and E. B. White

To state something precisely is to exactly do that. It is to define it sharply and minutely.

The precise meaning of words is influenced by the speaker's and the listener's backgrounds, experiences, and emotional state at the time. Also, the more abstract the word, the more varied its interpretation.

Here are a few examples of abstract words that invite multiple interpretations of their meanings: freedom, justice, patriotism, truth, honesty, soon, large, and beautiful.

The more precisely you can word your message the better you will be understood. Therefore, your goal should be to express yourself as exactly as possible. You want to leave no doubts in your listeners' minds as to what your comments mean.

Unfortunately, regardless of how precise your words are, there will be some difficulty in getting what you have said interpreted correctly. This uncertainty exists because of the differences in people, the nuances of language, and the fact that words are always only an approximation of the things and events they are describing (much like a map is only an approximation of the actual territory it represents).

Imprecise wording results from fuzzy thinking, saying the first word that pops into your mind, and the speaker's limited vocabulary. The first step in stating something precisely is thinking clearly about what you want to say. Next, you need to select the words that most accurately express the exact shade of meaning for what you want to convey and have your listeners hear.

You can improve your use of just the right word to get your message across by:

- Enlarging your vocabulary
- Looking up various synonyms that you can use and choosing the best one
- Using words that create mental images or pictures in people's minds of the thing or event being talked about (for example, the little red schoolhouse or the plain white church with the tall steeple on the village green)
- Thinking through exactly what you want to say before saying anything
- Knowing your listeners' backgrounds and experiences with the subject

Here are several examples that emphasize the differences between imprecise (I) and precise wording (P):

- I—I need the report as soon as possible.
  P—I need the weekly production report by noon today.
- I—I will be out of the office for several days next week.
  P—I will be in Tucson on Tuesday next week and will return to the office by one o'clock on Wednesday.
- I—While you are at the market, be sure to get something for lunch as well as some fish and dessert.
  P—When you go to Safeway, be sure to get one pound of provolone cheese and two pounds of hamburger for lunch, as well as two one-pound salmon steaks and a Pepperidge Farm coconut cake.

Use Specific Words

Be as specific as you possibly can when talking with people.

—Anonymous

Being specific is limiting or restricting what you are saying to a particular person, thing, or event. It is the opposite of being general or vague.

The more general and the less specific a word or phrase is, the more difficult it is to understand. Words work best when they convey specific meaning and worse when they are loaded with generalizations and ambiguities. By being specific you promote understanding and take much of the guesswork out of what you are saying. On the other hand, when you speak vaguely and in generalities, you cause confusion and create misunderstanding.

You can make your statements more specific and concrete if you do the following:

- Select your words carefully. Don't be content to settle for the first words that pop into your head.
- Use precise wording that conveys the exact information you want to share.
- Prefer language that is specific rather than general, concrete rather than vague, and tangible instead of abstract.
- Say words that create mental images or pictures in your listeners' minds.
- Refer to actual people, places, and events.
- Cite the names of people rather than using the pronouns he, she, and they.
- Give definite times and dates instead of approximations.
- Provide all the relevant facts and details without being excessive.
- State statistics and actual events to pin things down.
- Use several relevant examples and anecdotes.

Now let's look at a few examples that contrast general (G) and specific (S) wordings when communicating:

1. G—The child enjoys her soft toy.
   S—The two-year-old enjoys playing with her soft teddy bear.
2. G—The father and son went to the ballgame in the spring.

S—The father and his son Bill went to see a Dodger baseball game on the night of April 10th.

3. G—I need you to give this report a top priority.

S—I need you to get me the monthly financial report by noon tomorrow.

4. G—I need the project completed as soon as possible.

S—I need the Canfield project on my desk no later than 9:00 a.m. next Monday, November 1st.

5. G—Your monthly report was unsatisfactory and probably needs to be revised.

S—Section 4 of your monthly report needs to be more detailed before I can okay it.

Use Familiar Words

Every new movement or manifestation of human activity when unfamiliar in people's minds is sure to be misrepresented and misunderstood.

—Edward Carpenter

Familiar words and language are marked by informality. They are easily recognized by people. Familiar words are frequently said, heard, and experienced.

Your goal when speaking is to make your meaning instantly understandable. Don't force your listeners to exert a lot of effort to figure out what you are saying. It doesn't make sense to use words your listeners don't know. Remember, your purpose in communicating is to express not impress (people who really know a subject are able to use simple and plain words when talking about it).

Common sense dictates that you increase the possibility of being misunderstood when you use unfamiliar words and language. Also note that a word that is familiar to one person may not be familiar to other people. The sage Hippocrates once perceptively stated, "Nothing detracts from the clarity of language as much as the use of unfamiliar words."

Here are some tips on how to use familiar words and language that will help you to get understood:

- Use everyday words and phrases that people know and are comfortable with.
- Let short, familiar words convey how you think and feel about things.
- Show how your new ideas relate to ideas already known and familiar to your listeners.
- Use technical and specialized terms cautiously.
- Provide testimony and quotations from people your listeners know and respect.
- Cite examples associated with your listeners' backgrounds and experiences.
- Refrain from using foreign words, slang, clichés, or worn-out expressions such as

pretty as a picture	can't see the woods from the trees
the writing is on the wall	take to the woodshed
slow as molasses	chip off the old block
right as rain	sharp as a tack

Now let's examine how much clearer the meaning is with simple, familiar words contrasted with longer and unfamiliar words:

familiar	unfamiliar	familiar	unfamiliar
learned	erudite	enemy	protagonist
unnecessary	superfluous	extra	extraneous
neat	fastidious	aware	cognizant
small	diminutive	large	gargantuan
talkative	loquacious	excitable	exuberant
boundaries	parameters	generous	magnanimous
count	enumerate	benefactor	philanthropist
hungry	famished	sad	morose

This final thought from the Corinthians in the Bible emphasizes the importance of saying things plainly and in familiar terms:

Except ye utter by tongues
easy to be understood

how shall it be known what is spoken
for ye shall speak into the air

Use Gender-Neutral Words

*The differences in focus on messages and meta messages can give man
and women different points of view on almost any comment.*

—Deborah Tannen

Gender refers to a person's sex—male or female. Gender-neutral words
lack bias and prejudice—they don't favor one sex over the other.

Words can make a difference! They can create positive or negative
attitudes and feelings about people, things, and events. Historically, the
English language has been male oriented, favoring men and being biased
against women. Gender-neutral language treats men and women fairly
and as equals, whereas sexist language is biased against women. The frequent, even if inadvertent, use of sexist language can create relational
problems, interfere with understanding, and even cause resentment.

Effective speakers must acknowledge the existence of sexist language
and identify which words are sexist so they can avoid using them. They
also need to know how to use gender-neutral language so they can build
bridges rather than create barriers to understanding.

There is no denying that men and women communicate differently.
They have differing communications attitudes, perspectives, and styles.
Men and women could both benefit from learning how the other communicates. Knowing the similarities and differences could reduce misunderstanding. Recognizing that gender-biased language can upset people
and lead to misunderstanding, your goal should be to become aware of
what constitutes sexist language and to use gender-neutral (fair) words
routinely.

Here is a partial list of contrasting gender-neutral and sexist words.
There are many more gender-related words, but these examples should
suffice to make the point:

gender neutral	gender biased	gender neutral	gender biased
flight attendant	stewardess	firefighter	fireman
mail carrier	mailman	police officer	policeman

humankind	mankind	staffing	manning
sales rep	salesman	chairperson	chairman
engineer	lady engineer	woman	girl
executive	manager	women's college	girls' school
Miss Jones	honey	my secretary	my girl
nice appearance	sexy appearance	Mrs. Jones	Betty

Now let's take a look at some important differences that are generally present in most male-female communication that you should be aware of in order to improve your communication with the opposite sex:

- Women tend to talk on a more personal and emotional level whereas men tend to emphasize facts and downplay emotion.
- Men tend to make statements and lecture whereas women tend to listen and ask questions.
- Men tend to get right to the point and focus on solving problems while women tend to focus more on the process and details.
- Men typically don't listen as well and interrupt frequently. Women tend to listen better, interrupt less often, and provide more feedback.
- Men usually speak more directly or authoritatively and give orders. Conversely, women are more likely to make suggestions and be less direct and assertive.
- Men are commonly more competitive, disagree more often, and are more comfortable stating their opinions and arguing. Women tend to be more cooperative and more reluctant to disagree or argue.
- Men generally are concerned with maintaining their status in conversations while women are commonly more interested in connecting with others.
- Women tend to sit opposite each other in meeting settings and to look directly at each other, whereas men tend to sit at an angle and look at each other indirectly.
- Women tend to talk with some hesitation and a rising inflection in their voices, which suggests tentativeness and uncertainty to the men listening.

- Women are inclined to be more compassionate and politically correct when talking than are men.
- Men usually talk in generalities and abstractions whereas women stress tangibles and specifics (for example, women refer to their personal experiences more often than do men).
- Women tend to engage in small talk and chitchat while men are usually uncomfortable with and avoid this kind of talk.

Please note, much of this information is from Deborah Tannen's books on male-female communication. If you are especially interested in male-female communication, you may want to read her excellent books on this subject.

Use Technical Words Cautiously

A word whose meaning is perfectly clear to one person may be totally misunderstood by someone else.

—Anonymous

Technical language has special and unusual meaning and use. It is designed or fitted for one particular purpose, use, or occupation. It pertains to a specialized field of knowledge, such as science. Technical language is specialized with limited application.

Each science, technology, and occupation has developed its own distinct language to achieve an exactness or preciseness of expression that promotes understanding and discourages multiple meanings. Technical language promotes understanding by specialists in the same field but can't be readily understood by the average person.

Despite the potential communications barriers, there is a proper place for the use of specialized language and jargon. In many instances it is best for people in technical fields to employ highly specialized language because it offers a precision of meaning that might be lacking otherwise. When discussing especially significant matters, it is advisable to read the content of a technical subject word for word to minimize the possibility of it being misunderstood (and for the record). Try to use plain words and simple language whenever possible, and do your best to avoid using technical or specialized language with nonspecialists.

Fortunately, there are some countermeasures you can take to overcome problems caused by the use of technical language:

- Have ready access to and consult an up-to-date dictionary promptly when needed.
- Identify in advance the technical words and specialized language that you intend to use that may be new or unfamiliar to your listeners.
- Define unfamiliar technical terms at the beginning of your presentation.
- State things simply and briefly (use familiar language).
- Refrain from using acronyms and abbreviations, especially if they are not commonly known.
- Avoid using slang, colloquialisms, and foreign words.
- Watch for cues that indicate that your listeners are confused by what you are saying (e.g., facial expressions and body language).
- Stop immediately when your listeners appear lost; at this point ask for their questions or furnish additional information.
- Provide examples familiar to your listeners to make your point in a more concrete fashion.

Language is always in a state of flux. New words are constantly being introduced to the English language. Also, the meaning of existing words is changing continuously.

New words are usually associated with a new event, activity, or vocation. The following examples of the new terms being used in various fields should illustrate this point:

- Communications: fax, e-mail, the Internet, Kindle, Skype
- Computers: texting, website, Facebook, blog
- Space industry: liftoff, all systems go, mission scrubbed
- Transportation: jet lag, ground positioning system
- Medicine: body mass index, new labels and diseases (e.g., Alzheimer's, autism)

- Social activities: chill out, rapping, hang out, hook up
- Descriptions of people: spaced out, druggie, love child, wicked awesome

In addition to new words being misunderstood, further confusion results from the changing meaning of existing words. Here are several examples of common existing words whose meaning has changed drastically:

- Gay—from happy to male homosexual
- Partner—from business associate to persons of same sex living together
- Cool—from low temperature to impressive or good
- Challenged—from questioned or disputed to handicapped

In addition to single words, many new phrases are being used, such as:

- throw under the bus
- on the same page
- at the end of the day

The list of specialized words, new words, and words with a changed meaning is endless.

CHAPTER 6

Clarifying the Message

Think Before You Speak

It is necessary to think before speaking, but you must also think while speaking.

—Kenneth McFarland

When people think, they reflect on or ponder something. They consider and exercise judgment about a matter. Every communication begins with a thought. Clear thinking is the starting point for clear speaking. You can't expect something that is fuzzy and unclear in your own mind to be clear and coherent to the people listening to you.

Think about what you want to say and how you want to say it before you say anything important. By taking a little time initially to think over what you want to say, you may save substantial time later when you need to correct something ill advised that you said because you said it off the top of your head. A thoughtless comment is rarely effective and may prove to be disastrous. Remember, once you have uttered words you can't recall them (people may forgive something you said in haste that was offensive but they never forget being offended).

Before saying anything important it is a good idea to pause and ask yourself four questions:

1. What exactly do I want to say?
2. Why do I need to say it?
3. How can I say it most clearly and tactfully?
4. What will the listeners' reactions probably be?

The quality of your thinking depends on the quality of the information you have on the matter. The ideas you express can't be any better than the information you have available for forming your thoughts.

When you need to make an important presentation before a group you would be well advised to:

- Think about the topic for several days. During this time mull over different ideas and information that you would like to convey without making any decision about them at that time
- Determine your specific purpose and write it down in a brief statement
- Jot down your ideas on the topic freely as they come to mind without considering their importance, order, and relevance
- Research the topic to gather the best information from objective and reputable sources
- Analyze the data collected—keep only the most impressive information and discard the rest
- Develop your outline listing your main points in a logical sequence to guide your thinking (see Chapter 2 for details regarding organization)
- Determine the essential information and details you want to include to support your main points
- Think about your listeners. What are their expectations, attitudes, and understanding of your subject?
- Think about the key ideas you want to share and how to best word them
- Consider the probable questions you will be asked by your listeners
- Look up the proper pronunciation of any unfamiliar words you plan to say so you will know the right way to pronounce them
- Put away your outline and notes for several days without thinking about them
- Look over your outline and related information with a fresh outlook
- Finalize your preparation
- Think about the place where you will be delivering your talk
- Pause to think over your listeners' questions before answering them (it helps to repeat the questions aloud to make sure you understand them before responding)

This quotation by Pericles is worth remembering in this context: "The man who can think and does not know how to express what he thinks is at the level of him who cannot think."

Define Words

Define it well.

—Alfred Tennyson

A definition explains the essential meaning of words. It establishes boundary lines or determines the limits of meaning. Definitions attempt to create a common ground for communicating among different people, especially if they have widely divergent backgrounds.

No word means the same thing to any two people because the meaning of words is an intensely personal matter. Meaning exists only within a person and is always contextual. Humpty Dumpty made this point crystal clear when he said to Alice, "When I use a word it means what I want it to mean, neither more or less."

It is especially important to define words precisely when they possess several possible meanings or are technical in nature. For example, the words cat and run have dozens of possible meanings. Your goal when speaking is to use words that are as specific, clear, and familiar as possible.

It is helpful to get into the habit of consulting a dictionary whenever you want to pick the best word that says exactly what you want to say. However, remember that a dictionary has limitations. It only provides the general or usual meaning of a word at the time the dictionary was published. The words listed in a dictionary are constantly changing to reflect current word use. Also, over time the meanings of certain words change; for example, the current versus the previous meaning of such words as gay, partner, and liberal.

You can improve your ability to define words and expand your vocabulary through these behaviors:

- Have ready access to a current and reputable dictionary (preferably to a book of synonyms as well).
- Define all technical and specialized terms as well as words that are new or unfamiliar to your listeners (when in doubt

as to whether your listeners understand a word, be sure to define it).

- Offer synonyms when saying an unfamiliar word.
- Explain what a word is not or something that a word does not mean; for example, "By coexistence with Russia I don't mean appeasement" or "By compromise I don't mean capitulating or surrendering on key principles."
- Be careful not to talk down to people when defining a word or phrase.

Be Brief

Prune thou thy words.

—Cardinal Newman

To be brief is to be concise and of short duration. It is using few words and short sentences when saying something.

Your goal when speaking is to find the simplest, shortest, and most direct way to say something and yet to include all the necessary information. Your objective should be to find the right balance between being concise and being complete. It is a mistake to omit essential information just to be brief.

Your listeners appreciate it when you are brief. They can pay better attention and retain what you have said easier and longer when you are concise. Also, your main ideas stand out when you limit their number. An important part of being brief is knowing what not to say. And once you have decided on what to include in your message it is essential that you know when it is time to stop talking.

There are many ways you can be brief and thus enhance your chances of getting understood. Here are several of the best ones:

- Know your purpose and keep it constantly in mind.
- Limit information presented at one time to avoid overkill.
- Include only relevant and essential information.
- Cut out all unnecessary background and details.

- Eliminate all information already known or obvious to your listeners.
- Get directly to the point and stick to it—don't ramble.
- Use repetition only when it has a definite purpose.
- Use short words and sentences without being terse.
- Refrain from using nonessential modifiers (e.g., adjectives and adverbs).
- Stop immediately after saying what needs to be said.
- Cut out filler words that say nothing and waste time (e.g., uh, er, um, you know, like).
- Make every word count. Get rid of empty words at the end of sentences, such as these that say nothing: you know, and stuff like that, whatever, okay.
- Question the need for every word; when in doubt leave it out.

Omit a phrase when one word will suffice. Consider these examples:

because	due to the fact
if	in the event that
remember	don't forget
soon	in due course
although	in spite of the fact
please	we would ask that

Brief messages are often more powerful than long ones because the crux of the message doesn't get lost in a sea of words. The list of such powerful messages is endless. Here are several examples of powerful ones:

- The Lord's Prayer (from the Bible)—71 words
- The Ten Commandments (from the Bible)—297 words
- Lincoln's Gettysburg Address—271 words
- Marriage vows, "I do"—2 words
- Patrick Henry's "Give me liberty or give me death"—7 words
- I love you—3 words

Emphasize Important Information

Failure to emphasize any words or the wrong words robs your message of meaning.

—John Irwin and Marjorie Rosenberger

You emphasize something when you stress it or give it special importance. Stress is frequently used as a synonym for emphasis.

In any message, certain information is more important than other information. It is essential that you get your main points and central ideas clear in your own mind before sharing them with your listeners (you can't make clear to other people what isn't clear to you). Unless you emphasize which information is the most important, your listeners will tend to view all the information as equally important. To improve your chances of getting your key points understood you need to identify them for your listeners.

Fortunately, there are a number of excellent ways that you can use to stress your main points:

- Give important information more time than the less important information.
- Position your most important words and sentences at the beginning and ending of your comments (people remember best what you say at the start and finish of your talk).
- Limit the number of words regarding your main points so that they will not get lost in the midst of trivial details.
- Change your voice volume; vary your pitch level and tone of voice to stress something.
- Vary your rate of speaking. For example, talk more slowly when stating your main points.
- Pause to give your important ideas time to be absorbed.
- Use compatible facial expressions, body movement, and gestures to support your words.
- Reinforce crucial data by presenting it in more than one way. For example, compare and contrast using visuals or catchy words and memorable phrases.

- Cite relevant quotations and statistics pertaining to your main points to add punch.
- Ask rhetorical questions after saying something important—for example, "Now why is what I've said so important to your future?"
- Tell relevant anecdotes and stories that create greater interest.
- Cite examples and give complete explanations.
- Enumerate key points (e.g., add 1, 2, 3, 4 or a, b, c, d before each point).
- Repeat and restate major ideas with the same or different words and phrases to reinforce them in your listeners' minds.
- Offer periodic summaries of the main points, especially at the end of your presentation.
- Use picture words and visuals to accompany your words to pound important points home.
- Draw attention to your main points by saying, for example:
  o "Pay close attention to this point because …"
  o "Be sure to remember this …"
  o "Let me repeat this crucial point …"
  o "Now what I am about to say is the essence of my presentation, so listen carefully."

Make Definite Transitions

Tell them what you're going to tell them, tell them, and then tell them what you've told them.

—Anonymous

A transition is the passing from one subject to the next subject while speaking. Transitions are words and phrases that indicate when a speaker has completed one idea or point and is moving on to the next idea or point.

Transitions are necessary for you to get understood; their primary function is to alert the person listening that a new idea is being introduced. They are also used to hold a listener's interest. When you neglect to use proper transitions, you make it difficult for your listeners to follow the sequence of your thoughts.

Make your transitions as simple and smooth as possible (avoid abrupt or sudden transitions).

You may indicate transition by:

- Changing your voice tone or inflections
- Pausing between topics
- Gesturing and moving in a noticeable and meaningful manner (e.g., turning your head or body)
- Telling your listeners that you are moving to the next point

There are many words that you can say to show transition. These include:

furthermore	moreover	lastly
next	instead	but
in addition	meanwhile	conversely
consequently	again	similarly
therefore	finally	subsequently

There are also a number of phrases that you can use to indicate transition:

- On the other hand
- To sum this up
- Now, let's turn to my next point
- This brings me to my fourth point
- So much for the present, now let's examine the future
- We have listed the causes, now let's look at the possible solutions
- In conclusion

Use Repetition Properly

And oft repeated, they believe 'em.

—Matthew Prior

Repetition is the act of repeating. It is doing or saying something over, again, or several times.

There are two kinds of appropriate repetition:

1. Verbatim

    Verbatim is the repeating of a word or phrase using exactly the same words.

2. Paraphrasing

    Paraphrasing is the repeating of the same idea or information, but by using different words or phrases.

There are four legitimate purposes for repeating something:

- To clarify what was said
- To emphasize key information
- To give your listeners time to digest what was said
- To provide your listeners a second chance to hear what you've just finished saying in the event they were distracted by something while you were talking (e.g., a loud noise)

You should repeat words and phrases only when it serves a definite purpose. Useless repetition, if frequent, may bore your listeners and cause them to tune you out. Also, if you repeat something without a reason you may appear disorganized to your listeners.

Here is an example of a verbatim repetition contrasted with a paraphrased repetition, for the following statement: The Boston Red Sox welcomed the left-handed pitcher with great enthusiasm.

Verbatim: The Boston Red Sox welcomed the left-handed pitcher with great enthusiasm.

Paraphrased: The Boston Red Sox organization greeted their newly acquired southpaw hurler to the pitching staff with unrestrained exuberance.

Offer Appropriate Explanations

I wish he would explain his explanation.

—Samuel Johnson

To explain is to make known and understandable. It is to make something not immediately obvious comprehensible.

It is a good idea to explain anything that is new or complicated. You can't simply rely on a general statement and hope to be understood.

There are several things you can do to explain something to your listeners.

- Share experiences or do something together that is related to the information you are trying to get across.
- Review step by step a difficult procedure or process (e.g., assemble something or demonstrate how to do something, such as giving first aid or driving a car).
- Describe the details of something (e.g., route for a trip).
- Tell a story involving the ideas you are offering.
- Role-play a technique (e.g., holding a counseling session or managing conflict).
- Use the case-study approach, which involves considering all relevant factors when solving a problem.
- List the ingredients for making something (e.g., baking an apple pie).
- Draw a diagram or a map to visually depict what you are saying.
- Use a visual aid to present a mental image of something.
- Provide examples to make a generality or abstraction more clear, specific, and tangible.

Here are several examples that demonstrate how the use of examples can make a general point more clear and meaningful:

1. An increasing number of people are chronically ill. The number is rising because of an aging population, rapid changes in life cycle, obesity, lack of exercise, and pollution.
2. College costs are excessive and constantly rising (e.g., tuition is sky high, books cost hundreds of dollars, food and dorm costs are rising, and expensive loans are increasingly required).

3. People are reluctant to run for public offices because of the pressure and expenses involved. These include: excessive time demands, interruptions to family routine, personal attacks by the media, campaigning expenses, and the bitter political climate.

Provide Frequent Examples

Example is the school of mankind.

—Edmund Burke

An example is a brief reference to specific items or events. Examples clarify, reinforce, and personalize ideas. An example uses a specific case or instance to explain a general statement. Use examples to clarify or provide more information about something. By using examples you can minimize multiple interpretations of what you have said.

Remember that most people understand real-life examples better than they do hypothetical ones. The best examples are those that are familiar to and match the experiences of your listeners. Strive to support every new or complex idea with at least one example. This helps comprehension because examples often create word pictures for your listeners. Word pictures make generalities and abstractions more specific and concrete and therefore more easily understood.

Here are a few examples of how you can make generalities and abstractions clearer and easier to grasp (notice how each example clarifies the main point stated):

1. Many churches are in financial trouble and suffering because of this. (Example: More and more churches are closing, encountering staffing difficulties, and suffering from lower attendance.)
2. Feelings of patriotism are bolstered by symbols and rituals (examples: the Statue of Liberty, the Washington Monument, citing the pledge of allegiance, singing the national anthem).
3. People are increasingly upset with their medical care. (Example: The cost is ever increasing, there are long waits to see doctors, appointments are rushed, and insurance costs are high.)

4. Democracies are superior to dictatorship (examples: more freedom of expression and movement, greater economic opportunity, fair trials, free elections, less police brutality).

5. Recessions really harm people. (Example: People lose their homes, marital friction is created, people are depressed, and many people lose hope.)

Remember, the best examples are those that relate directly to the life experiences of the people listening to you.

Summarize Key Points

To summarize is a wise thing.

—Anonymous

You summarize a presentation when you succinctly review the main points stated. It is to sum up all that has been said that is especially noteworthy. Synonyms for summarizing are: an abridgment, an abstract, a synopsis.

Summaries are used as signposts to assist your listeners to see the overall picture of your presentation (by pulling all of the main points together). There are three kinds of summaries you can use: (1) preliminary, (2) periodic, and (3) final.

A preliminary summary occurs at the beginning of a presentation to provide an overview of the main points you are going to make in your talk.

The periodic summary occurs at different times throughout a presentation to remind the listeners of the main points that have been stated. It can also serve as a transition from the previously stated main point to the next main point. A periodic summary is often employed when a presentation is long or the subject is complex.

The final summary takes place during the concluding remarks. It reviews all of the main points addressed during the entire presentation.

Let's examine an example of each:

1. The Preliminary Summary
   Today my presentation will deal with the current recession. I shall be addressing four main points: (1) major causes of the recession, (2) problems created by the recession, (3) viable options to correct

the problems, and (4) the solution I recommend for overcoming the recession.

2. The Periodic Summary

   So far today I have talked with you about two of the four main points that I'll be addressing. First, I shared some ideas on the causes of the recession and second, I stated my thoughts on the problems caused by it. Now I'd like to identify several viable options for solving the problems.

3. The Final Summary

   Today I've shared my ideas with you on four points closely related to the recession. I began by listing the causes of recession (which were …). Next, I focused on the problems caused by it (such as …). My third main point identified possible options to correct the problems (which included …). And finally, I offered what I consider to be the best solution for ending the recession.

Note that the final summary should be brief and simply list the main points without any explanation.

Articulate Carefully

Active and energetic articulation is indispensable to good speech.
—John Irwin and Marjorie Rosenberger

Articulation is the making and joining of separate sounds to make words. It is the clear and effective utterance of speech sounds. In addition, it is the crispness and precision with which we form words vocally. The word enunciation is used interchangeably with articulation. Articulation occurs when the motion of the lips, tongue, and velum together with the pulsation of the chest muscles and diaphragm produces the sounds of speech.

Speech is basically an articulation process. Clear articulation is necessary to achieve understanding. Conversely, poor articulation interferes with getting understood and could make a person appear to be less intelligent than he or she really is. Your goal should be to make each sound distinct, precise, and easily intelligible. Try to attain a balance between overly precise and sloppy enunciation. Also, strive to sound natural when you talk.

Clear articulation doesn't just happen. You need to make a concerted effort to produce the various sounds precisely and correctly.

You can significantly improve your articulation by doing the following:

- Become aware of the things you are doing wrong. You can do this by:
  o Reading or talking aloud into a tape recorder and playing it back to learn how you sound to others
  o Watching yourself on videotape or in the mirror as you speak
  o Listening to especially articulate people to note how they speak and then comparing how they sound with how you sound
  o Consulting a speech therapist to discover your faults and to get suggestions on how to overcome them
- Make full use of your jaw, mouth, lips, tongue, and face muscles in tandem with proper breath control.
- Open your lips wide when you speak and move your jaw freely up and down (avoid being lip lazy).
- Relax your body, especially your larynx or voice box, and free it of tension.
- Improve your posture and breath control when talking.
- Keep your hands away from your mouth and chin while speaking.
- Produce each sound precisely by giving each vowel and consonant enough time (without sounding unnatural or stilted).
- Say entire words without substituting, adding, or dropping sounds (e.g., talkin' for talking, butta for butter, and sore for saw).
- Secure a list of tongue twisters and practice them to make your tongue more flexible and more easily movable.
- Avoid mumbling or swallowing sounds, which occur when you don't open your mouth wide enough when speaking or when the jaw is tight or tense (possibly due to stress).

Pronounce Words Correctly

Pronounce it faithfully.

—John Hay

Pronunciation is using the speech organs to produce words. It is how we say words. Your pronunciation of words affects your listeners' understanding immensely. Listeners are distracted, and even irritated, when they hear words mispronounced. Worse yet, your image and credibility may suffer when you don't say words correctly and distinctly.

It is important to realize that although most English words have only one correct pronunciation, many have an alternate acceptable pronunciation—for example, the words "either" and "route." In the final analysis, pronunciation patterns will be accepted if they coincide with those of the majority of educated people living in the community.

As a general rule, it is wise to use Standard American English pronunciation when speaking to U.S. audiences. Standard American English lacks the distinguishable speech characteristics of regional pronunciations. The preferred pronunciation can't be identified with a certain geographical region, such as Boston or Brooklyn. If you speak with a distinct dialect that is foreign to your listeners, you run the risk of setting yourself apart from them (whereas you really want to establish a feeling of commonality and togetherness with them).

Spellings of words in English are often different from the way they are pronounced. Thus, spelling can be misleading as far as correct pronunciation is concerned. Many words include a letter that is silent and should not be pronounced—for example, often, salmon, entrepreneur, indict.

On the other hand, some words include letters that should be pronounced but frequently are not—for example, February, library, poem, several. Still, other words are said incorrectly because a letter or syllable is wrongly added—for example, athalete, realitor, and idear.

A speaker's sloppiness or laziness when speaking accounts for additional mispronouncing of words; for example, thinkin' for thinking, goin' for going, ban for barn, and ca for car.

You can improve your pronunciation in several ways:

- Look up how to pronounce new words or words you are uncertain about in a current dictionary (dictionaries list the most popular or common ways of pronouncing words). Better yet, consult a dictionary specializing in American pronunciation of words, such as the one by Kenyon and Knott.
- Practice pronouncing new words until you feel comfortable when saying them.
- Pronounce a new word slowly, syllable by syllable (a syllable is a single uttered sound).
- Sound natural when you pronounce words (don't draw attention to the way you say things by being overly precise or by laboring with your pronunciation).
- Speak more slowly and distinctly when speaking to a group of listeners with different ethnic or cultural backgrounds.
- Refrain from adding sounds that say nothing when you are talking (e.g., ah, um, er).
- Substitute words that are easier to say when certain words give you trouble repeatedly. For example, use numbers instead of statistics.

Use Pauses Wisely

I do not understand, I pause; I explain.

—Michael De Montaigne

A pause is a temporary stop or a brief silence. It is a short period of time when no words are uttered.

There are several benefits you can derive from using pauses effectively. These include:

- Gives speaker a chance to think and thus present his/her thoughts in a more precise and organized manner
- Provides listeners with time to digest the new ideas or complicated information just heard
- Lets speaker appear to be carefully considering the next words he/she is going to utter

- Allows speaker time to look carefully at his/her listeners to gain feedback from their reactions to what he/she has just said before proceeding to the next point
- Permits the speaker to adjust his/her speaking style or content based on the feedback received
- Emphasizes the importance of the point just made
- Serves as a transition from one idea to the next
- Creates suspense as to what the speaker is going to say next

The number and length of pauses should vary according to the speaker's rate of speaking and the type of information being presented. For example, you may want to pause more frequently when sharing new, unfamiliar, or complicated information (or if you speak at a rapid pace).

In general, avoid too frequent or prolonged pauses. Unnatural pauses or undue hesitation can suggest to your listeners that you lack conviction or feel uncertain about what you are about to say.

In addition, try to eliminate the pauses caused by the use of ahs, ums, ers, you know, and other filler sounds or words, because they are meaningless, waste time, and cause distraction.

Use Body Language to Reinforce Words

Trust not a man's words if you please, or you may come to erroneous conclusions; but at all times place implicit confidence in a man's countenance in which there is no deceit.

—George Barrow

Body language is the movement of any part of the body to convey information as well as clarify and emphasize what is being said. Body language together with voice tone constitutes a person's nonverbal communication. Body language includes a person's appearance, facial expressions, gestures, posture, and movement of the head, shoulders, arms, hands, legs, feet, and torso.

Your body language plays an important role in your attempt to gain understanding. For example, less than 10 percent of communication that deals with feelings and attitudes is conveyed by words; the rest of the meaning comes from tone or other nonverbal cues.

It is important to note that your body language:

- Reflects your attitude and mental state intentionally or unintentionally
- Enriches or detracts from your verbal message
- Creates a reciprocal interaction with your listeners

In addition, your body language shows how you feel about (1) yourself, (2) your listeners, and (3) what you are saying.

Your facial expressions and other body movements have a language of their own. It is important to realize that your nonverbal behavior receives more attention than your verbal message. Body language can strengthen, weaken, or even contradict what you are saying. When your nonverbal language is consistent with your words, it makes your message more clear and easy to understand. Conversely, when it is inconsistent it causes the message to be mixed and difficult to decipher.

You will promote comprehension of what you are saying by using body language that is:

- Natural and spontaneous
- Purposeful rather than random
- Coordinated and consistent with the words you're uttering at the time
- Used judiciously rather than done to excess
- Timed optimally with what is being said
- Varied rather than repetitive
- Employed to clarify, emphasize, and reinforce the words being spoken

Try to refrain from using body language that is distracting and meaningless.

Since your body language is so important, it is essential you analyze it. You need to know what your body is doing when speaking and how it is influencing your listeners. This is not easy to do because people are not typically aware of what their body is doing while they are talking. You can gain some valuable insights from:

- Looking in a mirror while practicing your presentation
- Video-recording sample behavior while speaking
- Asking for objective feedback from people that you trust to tell you the truth

Understanding body language is difficult because it is extremely complicated and full of ambiguity. The same body language can be interpreted differently by different people at the same time. Its use and interpretation are strongly influenced by people's culture, prejudices, backgrounds, and so forth. Body language also occurs in a certain context. The bottom line is that you need to be cautious about the body language you use when speaking and when attempting to read your listeners' body language.

Secure Continuous Feedback

Men no longer test words to see what the truth is in them, the majority are only interested in knowing what their effect will be.

—Theodore Haecker

Feedback involves learning how effectively you have communicated. It is finding out how well your message has been understood. Feedback completes the communications loop between the sender (the speaker) and the receiver (the listener).

You can't merely assume that what you are saying is being understood—it is necessary for you to verify that what you have actually said is what you intended to say and that your message has been heard as you intended it to be heard. Give the obtaining of immediate feedback high priority when communicating so that you can correct any misunderstandings as they occur. Feedback provides your listeners the opportunity to make comments or ask questions about what you have said.

Fortunately, face-to-face communication furnishes you an excellent opportunity for securing instantaneous and continuous feedback from your listeners. Every listener sends out signals that disclose how your message is going over. These signals may be (1) verbal or nonverbal, (2) direct or indirect, or (3) conscious or unconscious (intentional or unintentional).

Let's examine some ways you can gain feedback:

- Desire to and actually work at getting feedback.
- State at the beginning of your talk that it is okay to interrupt you at any time to obtain clarification or more information. Also, make clear that there is no such thing as a dumb question and that it is permissible to offer personal opinions and differing views.
- Show your appreciation for all questions asked and avoid acting irritated with or defensive about any questions or comments.
- Maintain steady eye contact with your listeners to learn their reactions as you speak.
- Note the eye movements of your listeners (e.g., are they looking up or down, are they looking at you attentively or away from you with a bored look, or are their eyes alert or glazed over).
- Observe facial expressions or a lack of them.
- Be aware of your listeners' body posture (e.g., if they are fidgeting or slouched over).
- Watch movement of various body parts of your listeners (e.g., the hands and arms or legs and feet).
- Ask people to repeat the essence of what you have said in their own words.
- Say periodically, "I know you have some questions; what are they?"
- Pause occasionally to give listeners time to digest especially important information while at the same time leaning forward and looking around with an expectant expression on your face.
- Ask questions such as "What is your understanding of what I've just said?" or "What is your reaction to what I've just

spoken about?" or "What advantages and disadvantages can you see from what I've just proposed?"

- Respond to questions in an appreciative, nonjudgmental manner.
- Refrain from asking questions such as:
  - o Do you understand what I have just said?
  - o Do you agree with me that ...?
  - o What are your reasons for asking such a question?

State at the end of your comments that "now is a good time to ask questions; however, if some questions come to mind later, feel free to contact me about them."

CHAPTER 7

Speaking Voice and Style

Avoid Distracting Mannerisms

For a man by nothing is so well betrayed as by his manners.
—Edmund Spenser

A speaker's mannerisms are his or her adherence to a particular style or way of acting. Try to avoid any distinctive mannerisms that distract from what you are saying. Your goal is to get your listeners to focus on your message rather than you as the messenger. A distraction is anything that interferes with the listener's ability to concentrate on what you are saying.

There are all kinds of speaker mannerisms that interfere with a listener's ability to give full attention to what you are saying. These may be classified as: (1) attitude, (2) voice, (3) style of delivery, (4) body movement, and (5) use of language. Let's address each of these, starting with attitude.

1. Attitude:
   * acting either overly friendly (familiar) or detached (distant)
   * acting superior or condescending
   * acting too modest or humble
   * coming across as phony, unnatural, or "trying too hard"
   * appearing to be nervous, awed by or uncomfortable with the type of occasion or listeners
2. Voice:
   * talking either too loudly or softly
   * speaking with a rising inflection toward the end of sentences
   * dropping volume at the end of sentences
   * having a sing-song rhythm
   * speaking with an unpleasant tone (e.g., too shrill, husky, or breathy)
   * saying everything in a deadly monotone

3. Style of Delivery:
   - speaking either too fast or slow
   - hesitating too long between sentences
   - pausing awkwardly in the middle or sentences
   - pronouncing words either too precisely or sloppily
   - mispronouncing words or substituting sounds habitually (e.g., Calyfornia for California, sor for saw, or ca for car)
   - providing unnecessary detail
   - over- or understanding matters repeatedly
   - stating things implicitly and indirectly rather than explicitly and directly
   - overusing folksy and slang expressions
   - stating all important information in a tentative manner that suggests a lack of confidence or competence

4. Body Movement:
   - moving arms, hands, legs, and feet excessively and randomly
   - pacing around frequently without a purpose (like a caged lion)
   - breathing deeply and sighing often
   - shallow breathing causing a lack of breath or the end of sentences
   - blinking eyes rapidly
   - avoiding eye contact by looking up, down, or away
   - looking at listeners intently or slowly up and down their entire bodies
   - closing eyes for a prolonged period of time, especially during pauses
   - taking glasses on and off repeatedly
   - playing with eye glasses or looking over the top of them
   - smacking or licking lips while speaking
   - talking with hand on chin and bare movement of the lips
   - moving arms and gesturing in an aimless, repetitive fashion
   - massaging hands or arms, pulling on an ear, or rubbing of nose
   - making a pyramid of hands while making an important point and then speaking behind the pyramid

- moving hands and fingers nervously (e.g., shuffling papers, tapping with a pen, playing with coins or jewelry or with buttons on clothing)
- touching listeners' bodies frequently when talking to them

5. Use of Language:
  - repeating certain words and phrases excessively (e.g., you know, like, whatever, awesome, I have to tell you this)
  - making frequent and blatant grammatical errors
  - using tired and worn-out phrases such as "It doesn't take a rocket scientist to know…"
  - using fancy language to impress rather than express
  - using several words when one would suffice and long, complex sentences when shorter and simpler ones would be adequate

Act Natural

What is natural is never disgraceful.

—Euripides

When people act natural they are real, genuine, and authentic. They don't disguise or hide who they really are. A speaker is real when he or she talks naturally and sounds like himself or herself. You must be genuine to truly communicate. When you are speaking, you are continually sending signals (through your words, attitudes, and actions) that reveal who and what you are.

Your goal is to have your listeners view you as a genuine person who is a straight talker and who can be trusted. People need to trust you and believe that you are credible before they are able to believe what you say to them.

Listeners respect and admire speakers who have the courage to act natural and who are free of any affectation. Conversely, listeners are suspicious and resent speakers who are phony and try to "fake it."

You can convey that you are sincere, natural, and real in various ways, such as the following:

- Demonstrate a sense of being secure and not acting defensive.
- Disclose some personal things about yourself that show your listeners that you are willing to let them know the real you.

- Show the strength of your convictions by displaying some emotion while talking about a subject.
- Use words and phrases that you normally use.
- Gesture frequently, freely, and spontaneously.
- Speak with a voice tone that matches your real feelings and views about your topic.
- Match your facial expressions and body language with what is being uttered.
- Look and act relaxed and comfortable.

Get to and Stick to the Point

But still remember, if you mean to please, to press your point with modesty and ease.

—William Cowper

To get straight to the point means you immediately begin talking about the crux or essence of a matter. To stick to a point means you talk strictly and exclusively about matters relevant to the topic being discussed at the time.

Effective speakers get directly to the point and stick to it until all that needs to be said gets said. Your goal is to get the most out of a presentation in the least amount of time. You achieve this by concentrating on only one topic at a time, limiting comments to only relevant points and refraining from discussing whatever happens to come to mind at the time.

One effective way to get right to the point is to immediately state your purpose and then proceed directly to your first main point. In addition, it is wise to avoid having a lengthy introduction or offering excessive background information.

People are busy and are bombarded with heaps of information constantly. Therefore, they prefer and appreciate it when you get right to the crux of the subject. Conversely, they object and resent it when you waste time by taking all day to get to the essence of your presentation.

The crux or essence of a matter deals directly with the purpose of your talk. The crux of a problem involves three things:

1. Precise and clear description of the problem
2. Causes of the problem
3. Viable solutions to the problem

Now let's examine several important aspects of sticking to the point. Anything discussed should (1) be important and worthwhile, (2) be directly related to the topic, (3) make a difference, and (4) contribute to the discussion.

Regrettably, managing to get people to speak only about the matter currently being discussed is a constant battle because people like to ramble, digress, and go off on tangents. They typically have difficulty disciplining themselves by limiting their comments to the subject at hand.

These approaches have been found to be effective in helping people to stick to the point:

- Set and agree upon ground rules for the discussion (the do's and don'ts).
- Identify and clearly state the purpose of the discussion.
- Minimize conjecture, speculation, and stating mere opinion.
- Avoid excessive details, endless examples, and long explanations.
- Forbid "war stories" and all other interesting but irrelevant anecdotes.
- Focus on the present and future and not the past.
- To provide focus and to aid retention, use visual aids such as a PowerPoint presentation or a flip chart to list the key ideas/ points stated. A laser pointer can be used to highlight important points.
- Challenge in a definite but respectful manner anything being said that has been said before or that appears to be off target.
- Stop promptly when nothing new is being said.

Another effective approach to keeping on target is to put these questions on a flip chart or overhead projector in front of the group you are addressing to guide your discussion:

1. What are we doing right?
2. What do we need to do better?
3. What do we need to do differently?
4. What do we need to do faster or slower?
5. What do we need to do more or less of?
6. What do we need to stop doing?

When problem-solving, focusing on the following questions will aid the discussion by helping you to stick to the point.

- What exactly is the problem?
- What is the scope and seriousness of the problem?
- How long has the problem existed? (Is it getting better or worse?)
- When does the problem occur or what conditions or events appear to trigger the problem?
- What appear to be the major causes of the problem?
- Who appears to be involved in the problem and to what extent?
- What appear to be the consequences of the problem if it were to continue?
- What options are available for solving the problem?
- How can the chosen solution be implemented most effectively?

Speak in an Effective Style

Proper words in proper places marks the true definition of style.
—Jonathan Swift

A speaker's style is his or her distinctive manner of self-expression while speaking. It is the speaker's particular manner of saying or doing something. Speaking style includes such behaviors as:

rate of speaking	direct vs. indirect statements
type of body movements	formal vs. informal way of talking

confident-assured appearance	assertive vs. nonassertive demeanor
personal vs. impersonal comments	degree of listener involvement
use of notes and aids	flexible vs. inflexible attitude
voice variations	the way visual aids are used

Your communicating style affects your listeners' receptivity to what you are telling them. When a speaking style differs markedly from that which listeners are comfortable with, misunderstanding frequently occurs. Your listeners react to both what you say and how you say it. However, it is important for you to realize that as far as your listeners are concerned, how people say things (style) is generally more important than what they say (substance).

There is no one style that is recommended for all speakers. Your listeners, the subject, and the occasion all call for different speaking styles and approaches. Develop a speaking style that you are comfortable with and that works for you; and although it is best for you to develop your own style, it is worth noting that generally an informal, friendly, and open style is favored by most listeners.

Bottom line: Any style that helps you to say what you want to say and that assists your listeners to understand what you are saying is the right style for you to use.

Factors that affect a speaker's style are:

- Purpose of speaking
- Type of situation or occasion
- Subject and content
- Time available for presenting
- Type of seating arrangement (e.g., classroom or circular)
- Kind of setting and size of room
- Type of listeners
- Number of people present
- Personality of speaker
- Presenter's speaking skills and experience
- Type and amount of instructional aids to be used

Here are several ways that you can develop an effective speaking style:

- Observe the speaking styles of people who are effective speakers so that you become aware of what they do and don't do (but don't copy another person's style).
- Analyze your own speaking style by watching videos and listening to tapes of yourself speaking on various subjects.
- Ask for feedback from people who have heard you speak and who are willing to be frank with you (you can also pass out evaluation forms to your listeners at the conclusion of your presentations).
- Develop your own distinct style that is natural and comfortable for you and one that permits your personality to come through.
- Adapt your speaking style based on the listeners, subject, and occasion.
- Speak enthusiastically and in a conversational manner on most speaking occasions.
- Use lively language that appeals to your listeners.
- Practice speaking to develop and refine your skills (practice with different kinds of content as well as different rates of speaking).
- Consult with a speech expert to obtain the basics of effective speaking and read recommended literature addressing the fundamentals of public speaking (e.g., Effective Speaking by Dale Carnegie).
- Join a Toastmasters club.
- Avoid any annoying or distracting mannerisms, such as repetitive hand and arm movements, habitual facial expressions, or pacing around like a caged animal.

Use the Right Rate of Speaking

You should speak as rapidly as you can be clearly and comfortably understood.

—Kenneth McFarland

Your speaking rate is the speed or pace at which you speak. It is the number of words you speak within a certain time limit—usually the number of words spoken per minute.

Three factors determine your rate of speaking:

1. Type of subject matter (the content)
2. Time available for you to speak
3. Listeners' knowledge and interest in the topic

Strive to attain a happy medium between speaking too fast or too slow. It is unwise to say too much too fast. Conversely, if you talk too slowly you will bore your listeners and lose their attention. There is no single ideal rate of speaking. The general rule is to speak as rapidly as you comfortably can while still saying your words clearly and getting what you are saying understood.

It is normally best to speak at a moderate rate in a conversational style. People usually speak between 120 and 150 words per minute. You should try to speak at a rate of at least 120 words per minute. If you speak too fast, your listeners may view your speaking as impersonal and may think that you are unconcerned about your ability to be understood. (It is worth noting that some speakers speak too fast to be understood because the average listener can understand at a rate far faster than the average speaker can speak). Conversely, try to never speak at a rate slower than 100 words per minute or your listeners' attention will suffer.

Proper pauses can enhance understanding, whereas inappropriate pauses can create problems. Refrain from pausing in the middle of a thought; instead, wait until the end of the thought. Try to avoid prolonged pauses because they can interrupt the continuity of what you are saying; they can also suggest that you are uncertain about the next thing you want to say.

Proper pauses can be a huge plus. For example, they can:

- Emphasize your main points
- Give listeners time to reflect on what you've said
- Allow time for listeners to make comments or ask questions
- Serve as a transition between the last and next point

- Provide you time to organize your thoughts and search for the exact word you want to say next

(For more details on the use of the pause, refer to the section on pauses in Chapter 6.)

The following ideas should help you to speak at an effective rate:

- Speak more slowly when stating your key points to emphasize them and let them sink in.
- Speak more slowly when introducing new or especially difficult information.
- Talk at a faster rate when presenting details and less important information.
- State information familiar to listeners more quickly.
- Vary your pace to maintain interest.
- Speak at a rate that feels comfortable to you and that permits you to pronounce each word distinctly.
- Determine your speaking rate by timing yourself, preferably with a stopwatch, for a minute at time. Do this for the different kinds of content (write down the times to refer to later).
- Practice speaking until you are speaking at the desired rate.
- Time each practice session and record the actual time taken (do this for each major section of your talk).

Use an Appropriate Voice Tone that Is Consistent with the Message

Susceptible people are more affected by a change in tone than by unexpected words.

—George Elliot

The tone of a message expresses its attitudes, mood, or the emotions involved as revealed by its wording. Tone is hard to define precisely. It is an intangible that creates a certain feeling in the people listening to you. Your words can send one message and your voice something entirely different. For example, a person who has just received bad news may say "wonderful" or "great" with a serious and depressed tone of voice.

Your tone, or the overall feelings conveyed by your message, provides insights into your personality and your attitude toward your listeners and your subject. The tone also discloses your "between the lines" thinking about something.

A positive tone to a message is generally preferable to a negative one. A positive tone sounds cheerful, pleasant, and upbeat. On the other hand, a negative tone sounds pessimistic, skeptical, and full of doubt. Word things in a positive tone whenever you can. Listeners respond more favorably to positive messages. Positive messages encourage understanding, whereas negative messages encourage misunderstanding.

Negative words that you should avoid using include: no, won't, can't, impossible, fault, blame, wrong, disagreement, and foolish. Why? Because they frequently trigger an unfavorable reaction.

Let's look at a couple of examples of positive (P) and negative (N) ways of saying things:

1. (P) An employer enthusiastically presents an idea to his/her boss, which elicits this response "Thanks for your suggestion, I appreciate it. Let's see if we can find a way to use your idea."
   (N) "So, you have yet another idea, huh? The problem with your idea is that it is impractical why don't you get back to work?"
2. (P) A fellow is discussing the United States' chances in the Olympic Games with a friend and says, "I can't wait to see the Olympic Games on TV. I think we have an excellent chance to win the most gold medals because our athletes are much improved from the last games."
   (N) "I may watch the games on TV if there is nothing better to do. I'd like to see the Americans do well, but I don't have much hope because our athletes never seem to be in peak condition."

Tone your message in the way that is most appropriate for conveying your particular kind of information to a certain person or group. Normally, a friendly, warm tone to a message is more desirable than an impersonal, cold one. The tone of your message should be such that it sounds sincere and hopeful. It should always sound as though you are talking to an equal and never sound superior or condescending. You will create a more favorable tone to your message if you frequently use you, we, and us and rarely say I, me, and, my when speaking with people.

Now, let's turn to how voice tone influences the reception of what you say to people. Your tone of voice is important in setting the tone of your overall message. Your voice tone can give multiple meaning to what you are saying. For example, if you are talking about something serious, your voice tone should be solemn and deep. However, if you are saying something light and frivolous, your voice tone should have a lighter and lively tone to it. Speak in a confident tone of voice to make a good impression on people; however beware of sounding arrogant, superior, or demanding as this kind of voice tone alienates people and causes them to react negatively toward both you and your message. Also try to avoid habitually speaking in either a dull, bored voice or a high-pitched, excitable voice.

Frequently, people are unaware of their voice tone and how it affects others. Sometimes they may be aware that something about their message is being met with resistance and yet not have a clue as to what specifically is provoking such a negative reaction. It is vital to your success as a speaker (and as a person) that you pin down the exact nature of the problem

There are several things you can do to analyze your voice tone:

1. Record your voice and listen to it as attentively and objectively as possible.
2. Ask your friends and coworkers to give you honest and frank feedback on how your voice sounds to them (when you do this, be sure to express your appreciation for their candor and help).
3. Consult a speech specialist at a university or in private practice for his/her reactions and advice.
4. Consider your total personality, your basic attitudes toward life, and your relationships with people to gain additional insight.

It is wise to pay close attention to your voice tone because it reveals who you really are.

Speak with a Pleasant Voice Quality

So smooth, so sweet is thy voice.

—Robert Herrick

Voice quality is the overall sound of a person's voice. It is the combined characteristics of a voice that make it pleasant or unpleasant to listen to. Voice quality includes: the basic tone, pitch levels, resonance, clarity, and articulation.

Your voice is you. People judge you by the way you sound. Your voice quality is of prime importance in determining the impression you make on the people listening to you. Your voice should reflect the real you. It is the mirror of your basic personality, physical state, and mood at the time. Since your voice quality is so important, it is imperative that you gain insights into whether your listeners consider your voice to be pleasant or unpleasant.

Your listeners want to listen to a person with a pleasant voice that is free of annoying or distracting features. There is no doubt that people are more receptive to what you say when they like your voice and more resistant to your message when they don't like the sound of your voice.

Your goal should be to develop a pleasant, warm, and expressive voice. A pleasant voice originates from a relaxed chest, wide open lips, and a relaxed throat and neck. It has a clarity and purity of tone. In addition, the pitch level is neither too high nor too low.

A pleasant voice is free from breathiness and hoarseness, and it has neither too much nor too little nasal sound. Let's examine three key ingredients of voice quality: (1) breathing, (2) resonance, and (3) pitch:

1. Breathing

   Proper breathing is essential to good voice quality and projection. The source of energy for producing sound is the breath stream. Breath for speaking originates in the diaphragm. Speech occurs as breath is exhaled (your diaphragm supports your breath and your breath supports your voice).

   Your breath exhalation needs to be controlled, steady, and adequate. Your inhalation needs to be quick enough to avoid interrupting the continuity of your words. A sip of air is all that you need to utter long phrases. Whenever you inhale, be sure to do it silently without any tension in your neck or throat.

   Breathe often so that you will always have an ample reserve behind your vocal cords. If you run out of air, your volume at the end of sentences will be diminished and you may even drop your entire sentence endings. Your voice sounds old, weak, and tired when it is not supported by adequate air.

2. Resonance

Resonance is the vibration of the vocal cords, which then set the air within the resonators into vibration. The resonators determine the quality of your voice tone. A deeply resonant voice adds to the richness of the sound of your voice and is pleasant to listen to. (For example, voices of Tom Brokaw and Chris Wallace.)

The resonators modify and amplify the sound waves produced by the vocal cords. The main resonators are: (1) the throat, (2) the mouth, and (3) the nasal cavities. You can improve the resonance of your voice by:

- Singing
- Imitating the voices of radio or television announcer whose tone and resonance you admire
- Practicing lowering and deepening your voice tone and listening to how you sound on tape

3. Pitch

Pitch refers to both voice vocal range and inflection. The range is the difference between the highest and lowest pitch levels. Inflection is the pitch changes that make a voice interesting to listen to. Pitch is determined by the frequency of the vibrations of your vocal folds as you push air through them.

Strive to speak at a low pitch level most of the time. However, your pitch level should vary according to what you are saying at the time (more details regarding pitch are dealt with in the voice variety section of this book).

Fortunately, there are many ways you can improve the quality of your voice. It can definitely be improved with proper training and practice. However, you will need to make a strong commitment and concerted effort to improve it. It won't be easy nor will it happen instantly. By practicing recommended techniques you can improve the pitch level, volume, rate, variety, and overall quality of your speaking voice.

To improve your voice quality:

- Enroll in a public speaking course
- Join the Toastmasters Club in your area

- Secure and study videos of effective speaking and speakers
- Read an introductory speech text to acquaint yourself with the basic dos and don'ts
- Record your voice and listen critically to how you sound (identify your strengths and weaknesses and jot them down for reference)
- Ask your friends and business associates, who are willing to be frank with you, if they have noted any annoying voice mannerisms
- Speak in your natural voice unless it has defects
- Speak at a smooth-flowing rhythm and pace
- Talk with a moist, empty mouth
- Articulate distinctly; to improve tongue flexibility, practice tongue-twister exercises until you have mastered them
- Maintain a correct posture to aid your breathing and to feel relaxed; sit and stand tall-don't slouch
- Increase control of your breathing and airflow by breathing from deep within your diaphragm
- Breathe silently with quick, silent sips of air (especially if you are using a microphone)
- Keep your hands away from your jaw and mouth when talking
- Find and speak at your optimal pitch level
- Make proper use of your articulators
- Open your mouth wide and move your lips freely
- Relax and open your throat to minimize tension and encourage sufficient projection of your voice

Use Voice Variety

The voice so sweet, the words so fair, as some soft chime had stroked the air.

—Ben Johnson

Voice variety includes speaking with different sounds or changes in the voice. You achieve vocal variety by changes in volume, tone, and pitch level. Voice variety is a must. Unless you vary your voice you will bore your listeners, because you will be speaking without enthusiasm and in a monotone.

Voice variety offers several advantages:

- Creates interest
- Holds people's attention
- Emphasizes certain ideas and facts
- Expresses speaker's attitude and feelings at the time
- Promotes listeners' understanding

Any sentence can be said in a variety of ways by varying the rate, volume, and pitch level. It is a good idea to experiment with each of these factors to ascertain what works best for you.

We have addressed voice loudness and tone as well as speaking rate in previous sections of this book. However, not much has been stated about pitch so far. Therefore, let's now examine the various aspects of pitch in more detail. Pitch refers to both range and inflection. As mentioned previously, range is the difference between the highest and lowest pitch levels and inflection is the pitch changes, up and down, of your voice when speaking.

Vary your pitch optimally to be effective as a speaker. Changes in pitch level enable you to convey your feelings about a subject or situation. An expression and lively voice requires pitch variations. An effective speaker's pitch level moves up and down continuously in an infinite variety of patterns, much like a musical scale. It is best to use both high and low notes as appropriate, but use the in-between notes most of the time. Speak at a high pitch level to express excitement, enthusiasm, and lightheartedness. Speak at a low pitch level to express confidence and solemnity. The best pitch level to use depends on the nature of the subject and the type of occasion.

Most people prefer to listen to a pleasant, low-pitched (keyed) voice. On the other hand, they dislike listening to a high-pitched voice because this can be irritating and distracting. The use of a higher pitch at the end of a sentence can change a statement into a question and suggest uncertainty and a lack of confidence. In contrast, a habitual downward pitch can appear to be dogmatic and even aggressive. The habitual use of either too high or too low a pitch is ill advised.

Each person has an optimal pitch. This is the level at which the person's voice performs at its best. It is the tone that is most rich, full, and resonant. Your optimal pitch is one that is most comfortable for you and the one you speak in the most.

You can attain vocal variety by:

- Varying the loudness and softness of your voice
- Changing the pitch level based on the kind of words being spoken and the feelings the speaker has while saying the words
- Varying the quality of the voice (for example, stern to gentle)

Please note that the method of identifying your optimal pitch level is beyond the scope of this book but may be determined by consulting any good book on the fundamentals of public speaking.

Speak with Sufficient Loudness

Lo, he doth send out his voice; yea, and that a mighty voice.
—Book of Common Prayer

Loudness has to do with its intensity of sound or its volume. It refers to vocal audibility. It ranges from an extremely loud to an extremely low sound.

Your listeners can't understand what they can't hear. Your goal is to speak neither too loudly nor too softly. You need to speak loud enough to be heard easily yet not so loud that it is offensive. The loudness of your voice should vary according to:

- The subject you are talking about
- The sizes and acoustics of the room you're speaking in
- The number of people listening to you
- The type of seating arrangement

- The surrounding noise and types of distractions
- Whether or not you are using a microphone

It is important to realize three things about your voice volume:

1. Your voice sounds louder to you than it does to others because it reverberates inside your head.
2. Your listeners are more likely to tune you out if you speak too softly than they are to strain to hear what you are saying.
3. A loud voice is necessary for you to succeed as a speaker. For example, a loud voice makes you sound more confident and credible.

To create and maintain sufficient volume you need to:

- Breathe deeply from your diaphragm to fill your lungs with adequate air so you can project your voice powerfully
- Open your mouth enough to increase your resonance
- Open your mouth wide to speak without any obstructions
- Move your lips freely; avoid lazy lips
- Keep your mouth moist while speaking
- Stand or sit in an alert posture so you can breathe more easily
- Keep your hands away from your jaw and mouth so you won't stifle your words
- Remove gum or any other substance from your mouth while speaking
- Face your listeners constantly when speaking
- Record your normal speaking voice to discover how you sound to others (you don't sound the same to other people as you do to yourself)
- Test your speaking or microphone loudness to determine if everyone in the room can hear you easily (ask the people in the back of the room to raise their hands if they can hear you easily and ask the people up front if you are talking too loudly)
- Refrain from letting your voice trail off or fade at the end of your sentences

APPENDIX A

Self-Assessment of Skills Related to Getting What You Say Understood

Instructions: For each factor check the one column that best describes your attitude, knowledge, and action.

Always = A   Usually = U   Rarely = R   Never = N

	A	U	R	N
1. I think about what I am going to say before I say something.	A	U	R	N
2. When communicating I share complete, current, and accurate information with people.				
3. I share information in a timely manner.				
4. I adapt the content of my message to the kind of people I am talking with.				
5. I use body language to reinforce the words I am saying.				
6. I pronounce my words clearly, carefully, and correctly.				
7. My attitude and actions show that I like and respect people.				
8. I am aware of the needs and feelings of the people I talk with.				
9. My body language, voice tone, and words are consistent and all send the same message to people.				
10. My statements are brief and directly to the point without sounding abrupt.				
11. I say things in a candid, forthright, and straightforward manner.				
12. I say things briefly without omitting important information.				
13. I strive to achieve commonality and a sense of togetherness when talking with people.				

14. I say things in a way that is as concrete and specific as it can possibly be.				
15. I have the courage to say things that need to be said to people honestly without toning it down.				
16. I am aware of and respect the cultural differences among the people I talk with.				
17. I use familiar and commonly used words and avoid technical terms when speaking with people.				
18. I make a sincere and definite effort to get understood by people.				
19. I have and show empathy for the people that I communicate with.				
20. I minimize using politically correct language.				
21. I am enthusiastic when conversing with people.				
22. I use frequent and relevant examples when explaining things to people.				
23. I have realistic expectations for getting what I say understood.				
24. I say things in an explicit way to people.				
25. I use gender-neutral and fair language when talking with people.				
26. I seek prompt feedback to ensure that what I said was understood.				
27. I use correct grammar when speaking with people.				
28. I limit the amount of information that I share with people at any one time.				
29. I make a consistent and definite effort to say things in an interesting manner.				
30. I realize people have short attention spans and that I need to work to retain their attention.				
31. I know that I must show an interest in the people listening to me for them to want to listen to me.				
32. I avoid having mannerisms when speaking that are distracting or annoying to people.				
33. I act genuine and natural when interacting with people.				
34. I share my thoughts in an organized manner and in a logical sequence.				
35. I get directly to the point and stick to it when speaking with people.				
36. I use precise words and say exactly what I intend to say to people.				

37. I know and state my specific purpose for talking with people about important matters.				
38. I establish rapport quickly with the people I am talking with.				
39. I vary my rate of speaking depending on the type of content and people listening to me.				
40. I include only important information and omit unimportant information when talking with people.				
41. I repeat information in different words to help me get understood.				
42. I use simple words and plain language when speaking with people.				
43. I am sincere and demonstrate my sincerity when I say something.				
44. I summarize important points when talking at length on a topic.				
45. I am both tactful and truthful when I talk with people.				
46. I select the best time for both myself and others when I plan to talk with them about important matters.				
47. I make clear and definite transitions when speaking about something important.				
48. I speak loudly enough for people to hear me easily.				
49. I try to develop a large vocabulary so that I can express myself more exactly.				
50. I realize that words have different meanings to different people and I act accordingly when talking with people.				

Scoring Instructions: Check to see that you have answered all 50 questions. Give yourself 4 points for every Always answer, 3 points for Usually, 2 points for Rarely, and 1 point for Never. Add up all your points.

Scoring Scale

180–200 points = excellent   160–179 = superior

140–159 = satisfactory   0–139 = unsatisfactory

My Total Points =

APPENDIX B

Self-Assessment of Skills Related to Understanding What Is Said to You

Instructions: check the one column that best describes your attitude, knowledge, and action for each factor listed:

Always = A Usually = U Rarely = R Never = N

	A	U	R	N
1. I avoid letting a person's appearance distract me from what he/she is saying.				
2. I give my full attention to what people are saying to me.				
3. I have an open-minded and receptive attitude about what a person is saying to me.				
4. I am aware that the same word can have different meanings to different people.				
5. I avoid prejudging or jumping to conclusions regarding what people are saying to me.				
6. I observe the body language of people to help me understand what they are saying.				
7. I read between the lines to help me understand what a person is really saying.				
8. I listen carefully to identify the main ideas being stated by a person.				
9. I distinguish between fact, inference, and opinion when a person is talking to me.				
10. I encourage people to speak candidly with me.				
11. When something is said that is unclear to me, I ask questions to clarify what the person has said.				
12. I am alert to the mixed signals conveyed by the person speaking to me.				

13. I make a strong effort to understand what a person is saying to me.				
14. I study the context in which a statement is made to help me understand what it means.				
15. I listen objectively to what people say to me.				
16. I ask the person speaking to define unfamiliar words or technical terms for me.				
17. I consider the cultural background of the person speaking when interpreting what he/she is saying.				
18. I ask people to explain things they say to me so that I can understand them.				
19. I avoid being distracted by a person's inflammatory or highly emotional language.			.	
20. I realize that I can absorb only a limited amount of information at one time.				
21. I recognize my emotional blind spots and prejudices regarding people, beliefs, and things.				
22. I avoid discussing important matters when I am preoccupied, tired, or not feeling well.				
23. I avoid taking mental vacations or when they are talking with me.				
24. I pay special attention to a speaker's introductory and concluding comments when listening to a presentation.				
25. I do my best to maintain interest in what people are saying to me.				
26. I notice whether the person speaking habitually uses words that overstate or understate things.				
27. I try to learn the purpose of why a person is discussing a particular subject with me.				
28. I identify the speaker's transitions as he/she moves from one topic to the next.				
29. I pay more attention to a speaker's content than to his/her style of speaking.				
30. I allocate adequate time to discuss important matters with people.				
31. I listen to a person's voice tone as well as the content of what he/she is saying to me.				
32. I have developed a large vocabulary to help me understand what is said to me.				

33. I pay close attention to a speaker's choice of words.				
34. I notice when people use vague or self-protective words to qualify the meaning of what they are saying.				
35. I avoid being unduly influenced by the quality of a person's voice.				
36. I attempt to determine the credibility and sincerity of the people I talk with.				
37. I select a private and quiet place to hold important discussions.				
38. I avoid being unduly influenced by a speaker's big words and fancy language.				
39. I have the courage to let people be frank and level with me.				
40. I look up the meaning of new words when I hear them.				
41. I try to determine if a speaker's information is current, complete, and accurate.				
42. I try to identify the biases and motivations of people I talk with.				
43. I sit or stand in an alert but comfortable position when discussing something important.				
44. I know my listening strengths and weaknesses.				
45. I ask people to get to and stick to the point when they start to ramble.				
46. I avoid letting a person's use of incorrect grammar distract me from hearing what he/she is saying.				
47. I help people I am talking with to relax and feel at ease.				
48. I notice when the person speaking pauses or changes pitch level, volume, or rate of speaking.				
49. I provide prompt and ongoing feedback while I listen to a person talking.				
50. I listen closely to the total person (words, voice tone, and body language) to help me understand what is being said.				

Scoring Instructions: Check to see that you have answered all 50 questions. Give yourself 4 points for every Always answer, 3 points for Usually, 2 points for Rarely, and 1 point for Never. Add up all your points.

Scoring Scale

180–200 points = excellent   160–179 points = superior

140–159 points = satisfactory   0–139 points = unsatisfactory

My Total Points =

About the Author

Walter St. John is a semiretired writer with management experience in both private and public sectors as well as serving as an officer in the U.S. Army. He and his wife and dogs live in the outskirts of Bangor, Maine.

His education includes a BA Degree in Speech and Communications, a Master's Degree in Political Science, both from the University of Arizona, and a Doctorate in Management and Counseling from the University of Southern California.

Dr St. John's career includes being an executive with the Hershey Company, Director of Program and Services for a National Food Trade Association—NYC, a Principal and a Superintendent of Schools, Assistant Vice Chancellor of a State University, and President of the Management Communication Institute.

Index

abstract words, 39–40
accurate information, 40–42
act natural, 99–100
adapting, content, 35–36
amount of information, 38–39
appropriate repetition, 83
articulation, 87–88
attention, 23–25
attitude, 4–5
  mannerisms, 97
awareness, 7–8

body language. *See also* language
  cultural differences, 48
  to reinforce words, 91–93
body movement, mannerisms, 98–99
breathing, voice quality, 109–110
briefing, 78–79

candid, 9–11
cautions, word meanings, 58–60
clarifying the message
  articulation, 87–88
  body language, 91–93
  brief, 78–79
  emphasizing, 80–81
  examples, 85–86
  explanation, 83–85
  feedback, 93–95
  pauses, 90–91
  pronunciation, 89–90
  repetition, 82–83
  summarizing, 86–87
  thinking, 75–77
  transition, 81–82
  words, definition, 77–78
clarity, 61–63
colors and numbers, cultural
    differences, 49
commonality, 2–3
common sense, 68

communication
  eight-C's octagon of, 33
  male-female, 71–72
  style, 103
complete information, 36–37
comprehension, 85, 92
conclusion, 31–32
concrete words, 39–40
confidence, 5
  projection of, 17
connecting, communication, 71
consistent message, 42–43
content of message
  accurate information, 40–42
  adapting, 35–36
  amount of information, 38–39
  complete information, 36–37
  concrete words, 39–40
  consistent message, 42–43
  eight-C's octagon, 33
  interest, 33–35
  relevant information, 37–38
context of message
  culture, 46–50
  definition, 45
  meaning of words, 45–46
  time, 50–53
courage, 11–13
credibility, 16–17
crux of problem, 100–101
cultural differences, 47–49
culture, 46–50

desire to understood, 5–6
dictionary, 56
distraction, mannerisms, 97–99
doublespeak, words, 63

effort to understand, 6
eight-C's octagon, 33
empathy, 8–9

emphasizing, 80–81
enthusiasm, 22–23
ethnic and racial, cultural differences, 47
euphemisms, words, 63
examples, 85–86
explanations, 83–85

familiar words and language, 68–70
feedback, 93–95
feelings and empathy, 9
final summary, 87

gender
    cultural differences, 47
gender-neutral language, 70
gender-neutral words, 70–72

imprecise wording, 65–66
information
    accurate, 40–42
    amount of, 38–39
    complete, 36–37
    relevant, 37–38
interest, 33–35
introduction, 30–31

language. *See also* body language; words
    body, 48
    cultural differences, 48
    familiar, 68–70
    gender-neutral, 70–72
    mannerisms, 99
    technical, 72–74
loudness, 113–114

mannerisms, 97–99
meanings, word, 58–60
message, tone of, 106–108

organization of message
    conclusion, 31–32
    introduction, 30–31
    planning and organizing, 28–30
    responsibility, 27–28
organizing, planning and, 28–30

paraphrasing repetition, 83
pauses, 90–91
perception, 7, 8
periodic summary, 87
personality traits
    appealing, 1–2
    attention, 23–25
    attitude, 4–5
    awareness, 7–8
    candid, 9–11
    characteristics, 2
    commonality, 2–3
    courage, 11–13
    credibility, 16–17
    effort to understand, 6
    empathy, 8–9
    enthusiasm, 22–23
    rapport, 14–16
    reciprocate, 20–22
    sincerity, 13–14
    strength to understanding, 5–6
    tactful, 17–19
    trust, 19–20
pitch, voice quality, 110–111
planning and organizing, 28–30
pleasant voice, 108–111
point, getting and sticking, 100–102
political correctness, words, 63
positive thinking, 4
precise words, 65–66
preliminary summary, 86–87
problem, crux of, 100–101
pronunciation, 89–90

quality, voice, 108–111

rapport, 14–16
rating, speaking, 104–106
reciprocate, 20–22
regional, cultural differences, 48
reinforce words, body language to, 91–93
relationships, 14
relevant information, 37–38
religious, cultural differences, 48
repetition, 82–83
resonance, voice quality, 110
responsibility, 27–28

simple words, 63–65
sincerity, 13–14
space, cultural differences, 48–49
speaking voice and style
    act natural, 99–100
    effective style, 102–104
    loudness, 113–114
    mannerisms, 97–99
    pleasant voice, 108–111
    point, getting and sticking,
        100–102
    rating, 104–106
    tone, 106–108
    voice variety, 111–113
specific words, 66–68
style, 102–104. *See also* voice and style
style of delivery, mannerisms, 98
sufficient time, 50–53
summarizing, 86–87

tactful, 17–19
technical words and language, 72–74
thinking, 75–77
time
    cultural differences, 49
    sufficient, 50–53
tone, 106–108
traits. *See* personality traits
transition, 81–82
trust, 19–20

understanding
    cultural differences, 49–50
    effort to, 6, 21–22
    strength to, 5–6

verbatim repetition, 83
vocabulary, 55–56
    behaviors, 77–78
voice
    cultural differences, 48
    mannerisms, 97
    pleasant, 108–111
    variety, 111–113
voice and style
    act natural, 99–100
    effective style, 102–104
    loudness, 113–114
    mannerisms, 97–99
    pleasant voice, 108–111
    point, getting and sticking,
        100–102
    rating, 104–106
    tone, 106–108
    voice variety, 111–113

words. *See also* language
    body language to, 91–93
    causes of, 60
    choice of, 57–58
    clarity, 61–63
    concrete, 39–40
    definition, 77–78
    familiar, 68–70
    gender-neutral, 70–72
    meaning of, 45–46, 59–60
    precise, 65–66
    simple, 63–65
    specific, 66–68
    technical, 72–74
    vocabulary, 55–56

OTHER TITLES IN OUR CORPORATE COMMUNICATION COLLECTION

Debbie DuFrene, Stephen F. Austin State University, Editor

- *The Presentation Book for Senior Managers: An Essential Step by Step Guide to Structuring and Delivering Effective Speeches* by Jay Surti
- *Communicating to Lead and Motivate* by William C. Sharbrough
- *Public Speaking Kaleidoscope* by Rakesh Godhwani
- *Essential Communications Skills for Managers, Volume I: A Practical Guide for Communicating Effectively with All People in All Situations* by Walter St. John and Ben Haskell
- *How to Write Brilliant Business Blogs, Volume I: The Skills and Techniques You Need* by Suzan St. Maur
- *How to Write Brilliant Business Blogs, Volume II: What to Write About* by Suzan St. Maur
- *Managerial Communication and the Brain: Applying Neuroscience to Leadership Practices* by Dirk Remley
- *Essential Communications Skills for Managers, Volume II: A Practical Guide for Communicating Effectively with All People in All Situations* by Walter St. John and Ben Haskell
- *Producing Written and Oral Business Reports: Formatting, Illustrating, and Presenting* by Dorinda Clippinger

Announcing the Business Expert Press Digital Library

Concise e-books business students need for classroom and research

This book can also be purchased in an e-book collection by your library as

- a one-time purchase,
- that is owned forever,
- allows for simultaneous readers,
- has no restrictions on printing, and
- can be downloaded as PDFs from within the library community.

Our digital library collections are a great solution to beat the rising cost of textbooks. E-books can be loaded into their course management systems or onto students' e-book readers.
The **Business Expert Press** digital libraries are very affordable, with no obligation to buy in future years. For more information, please visit **www.businessexpertpress.com/librarians**. To set up a trial in the United States, please email **sales@businessexpertpress.com**.

www.ingramcontent.com/pod-product-compliance
Lightning Source LLC
Chambersburg PA
CBHW062013200326
41519CB00017B/4789